ALICE, GRAND |

PRI

GREAT BRITAIN AND IRELAND

LETTERS

TO HER MAJESTY THE QUEEN

WITH A MEMOIR

BY H.R.H. PRINCESS CHRISTIAN

Volume II

Elibron Classics
www.elibron.com

COLLECTION

OF

BRITISH AUTHORS

TAUCHNITZ EDITION.

VOL. 2349.

ALICE, GRAND DUCHESS OF HESSE

IN TWO VOLUMES.

VOL. 2.

LEIPZIG: BERNHARD TAUCHNITZ.

PARIS: C. REINWALD, 15, RUE DES SAINTS PÈRES.

PARIS: THE GALIGNANI LIBRARY, 224, RUE DE RIVOLI,
AND AT NICE, 15, QUAI MASSENA.

COLLECTION

OF

BRITISH AUTHORS

TAUCHNITZ EDITION.

VOL. 2349.

ALICE, GRAND DUCHESS OF HESSE.

IN TWO VOLUMES.—VOL. II.

ALICE

GRAND DUCHESS OF HESSE

PRINCESS

OF

GREAT BRITAIN AND IRELAND.

LETTERS TO HER MAJESTY THE QUEEN.

WITH

A MEMOIR BY H.R.H. PRINCESS CHRISTIAN.

COPYRIGHT EDITION.

IN TWO VOLUMES.—VOL. II.

LEIPZIG

BERNHARD TAUCHNITZ

1885.

CONTENTS

OF VOLUME II.

——

1867.

1868.

1869.

LETTERS.

(CONTINUED.)

1867.

(CONTINUED.)

Darmstadt: September 8.

. . . I spent three days and two nights with dear Alix at Wiesbaden, and I find her leg decidedly better. . . . It is a little less hot to-day, but much hotter even now than we ever have it in England. Stallmeister Meyer* came to see us yesterday, and we took him out riding, which made him quite happy. Anyone who reminds me of the good old times before the 14th of December does me good; it is a pleasure to speak about those past so happy days! When they came to a close, I lost the greater part of my joyousness, which, though I am so happy, has never returned. A certain melancholy and sadness sometimes overcome me, which I can't shake off; then I have *Heimweh* after adored Papa to such an extent that tears are my only relief.

---

* Riding-master to the Prince Consort and the Queen from 1840 to 1871.

Darmstadt: October 3.

Yesterday evening I returned from Wiesbaden, leaving Alix well, but having caught a bad cold myself. The children have equally heavy ones.

Darmstadt: October 8.

Many thanks for your letter just received, and for the review of dear Papa's Life, which is excellent, and which I sent on to Aunt Feodore, as you desired. I have been laid up for a week with influenza, and am only about again since yesterday, though not out of the house. I am quite weak from it. The whole house is laid up with bad colds, and Baby can't shake hers off at all. The cough is so tiring, and she whoops whenever she coughs. Poor Jäger, who is, alas! we fear, consumptive, broke a blood-vessel two days ago, and is dangerously ill, to the great grief of all in the house. He is our best servant, and so devoted; he never would take care of himself, as he could not bear letting anyone but himself attend on Louis. We have just got a *Diakonissin* [Deaconess] to nurse him; on account of his great weakness he can't be left alone one instant.

Sir William, Lady and Charlotte Knollys have been on a visit to us; also Lady Geraldine Somerset for two nights. They are all interested to see our house.

Uncle George has made me a present of one of the horses the Sultan sent him.

Darmstadt: October 10.

I can't find words to say how sorry I am that dear sweet Arthur should have the small-pox! and that you should have this great anxiety and worry. God grant, that the dear boy may get well over it, and that his dear handsome face be not marked! Where in the world could he have caught it? The Major kindly telegraphs daily, and you can fancy, far away, how anxious one is. I shall be very anxious to get a letter with accounts, for I think constantly of him, and of you. My parents-in-law wish me to tell you how they share your anxiety, and how they wish soon to hear of dear Arthur's convalescence; of course my Louis likewise, for he shares all my feelings, being a real brother towards my *Geschwister* [brothers and sisters].

Darmstadt: October 14.

How glad I am to see by your letter that darling Arthur is going on so very well! One can't be too thankful; and it is a good thing over, and will

spare one's being anxious about him on other
occasions.

Bertie and Alix have been here since Saturday
afternoon, and leave to-morrow. They go straight
to Antwerp, and Bertie is going back to Brussels to
see the cousins.

The visit of the King went off very well, and
Alix was pleased with the kindness and civility of
the King. I hear that the meeting was satisfactory
to both parties, which I am heartily glad of. Bearing ill will is always a mistake, besides its not
being right.

Dear Alix walked up our staircase with two
sticks, of course very slowly, but she is improving
wonderfully, though her knee is quite stiff.

Poor Jäger is a little better, and the momentary
danger is past, though I fear he cannot ultimately
recover. How hard for poor Katrinchen! There is
much sorrow in the world, and how often such a
share falls to the best and gentlest! I of course go
to see him daily, but it always goes to my very
heart to see that attached and faithful creature dying slowly away. How is Brown's sister?

We hope that Countess Blücher will return here
with Vicky and me from Baden for a few days, as
it is an age since Vicky has seen her.

Dear Alix is writing in my room at this moment,

and is so dear and sweet. She is a most loveable creature.

Darmstadt: October 23.

The accounts of poor dear Aunt Feodore are so sad, and I hear she does not look well, and is so low about her eyes.

Schweinsberg: October 24.

Dear Vicky and Fritz left us yesterday morning. It is such a pleasure to me to think that they, like Bertie and Alix, know my house, and that they have lodged under our roof. When will you, darling Mama? If ever again you go abroad and wish to rest on your way, all in the world we have is at your disposal. How happy that would make us!

We ourselves left at four yesterday afternoon, remaining the night at Marburg, and leaving at a quarter to five in the morning, so that Louis could reach Alsfeld in time to join the shooting-party. We parted at Kirchhain, and I came here with Christa to her mother's house—so sad and changed since three years ago. It is most kind of them to have taken me up here, and the bracing air will do me good. They know that I can understand what a house of mourning is, and that I don't want to amuse myself.

Ella cried on parting with us yesterday, and wanted to get into the train with us.

Victoria is going to have a little lesson every other day, when I go back, from Mr. Geyer, who taught poor Willem, and who teaches little girls particularly well. She must begin in my room, as it is better not to have lessons in the nursery, I think. Vicky and I spoke much together about education and taking a governess. I thought to wait a year (for financial reasons), and I think it time enough then—do not you?

November 15.

. . . It is so good and wholesome not always to be one's own master, and to have to suit oneself to the wish of others, and, above all, to that of one's mother and sovereign. —— feels it as such, and often told me so, regretting how seldom such was the case.

The Moriers are often with us, and we value them much; they are such pleasant companions, and such excellent, clever people.

Darmstadt: December 6.

. . . The visit to Claremont must have been quite peculiar for you; and I can fancy it bringing back to your mind the recollections of your childhood.

In spring it must be a lovely place, and, with gayer papers on the walls, and a little modern comfort, the house must likewise be very pleasant. Ella, who was breakfasting with me just now, saw me dip my *Bretzel* in my coffee, and said: "Oh, Mama, you must not! Do you allow yourself to do that?" because I don't allow her to do it. She is too funny, and by no means quite easy to manage—a great contrast to Victoria, who is a very tractable child. Ella has a wonderful talent for sewing, and, when she keeps quiet a little while, sews quite alone and without mistakes. She is making something for you for Christmas, which she is quite excited about. Victoria's little afternoon lesson answers admirably, and is the happiest time of the day for her. She can read words already.

We have snow and ice, and no sunshine since some time, and it is not inviting to take the dull walks in the town. But I make a rule to go out twice a day, and keep nearly the same hours as at home.

The account of your visit to Lady Palmerston and to her daughter is most touching. It is so inexpressibly sad for grandmother and mother, for it is unnatural for parents to survive their children, and that makes the grief a so peculiar one, and very hard to bear.

December 9.

. . . During the long winter days, when Louis is away sometimes four times in the week from six in the morning till six in the evening, and then when he returns from his shooting has his work to do, I feel lonely. I am often for several hours consecutively quite by myself; and for my meals and walks only a lady, as she is the only person in the house besides ourselves. It is during these hours, when one cannot always be reading or at work, that I should wish to have some one to go to, or to come to me to sit and speak with; but such is not the case, and it is this I regret—accustomed as I was to a house full of people, with brothers and sisters, and, above all, the chance of being near you. I always feel how willingly I would spend some of those hours with or near you—and the sea ever lies between us! When Louis is at home and free—for in the morning I don't see him—then I have *all* that this world can give me, for I am indeed never happier than at his dear side; and time only increases our affection, and binds us closer to each other.

We have deep snow now and sledging the last two days.

December 12.

Before going to rest, I take up my pen to write

a few loving words, that they may reach you on the
morning of the 14th. The sound of that date brings
with it that sad and dreary recollection which, for
you, my poor dear Mama, and for us, time cannot
alter. As long as our lives last, this time of year
must fill us with sad and earnest feelings, and re-
vive the pain of that bitter parting.

I ought not to dwell on those hours now, for it
is wrong to open those wounds afresh, which God
in His mercy finds little ways and means to heal
and soothe the pain of.

Dear darling Papa is, and ever will be, *immortal.*
The good he has done; the great ideas he has pro-
mulgated in the world; the noble and unselfish example he has given, will live on, as I am sure he
must ever do, as one of the best, purest, most God-
like men that have come down into this world. His
example will, and does, stimulate others to higher
and purer aims; and I am convinced that darling
Papa did not live in vain! His great mission was
done; and what has remained undone he has placed
in your dear hands, who will know best how to
achieve his great works of love and justice. I shall
think much, very much, of you on the 14th, and you
will be more in my prayers than ever. Think also
a little of your most devoted child!

Darmstadt: Christmas Day.

We missed poor Willem so much in arranging
all the things; and poor Jäger's illness was also sad.
We gave him a tree in his room. He looks like a
shadow, and his voice is quite hoarse.

To two hospitals, the military and the town one,
I took presents yesterday, and saw many a scene of
suffering and grief. My children are going to give
a certain number of poor children a *Bescheerung* on
New Year's Day. It is so good to teach them early
to be generous and kind to the poor. They even
wish to give some of their own things, and such as
are *not* broken.

Your many generous presents will find their use
at once, and the Christmas pie, &c., be shared by
all the family. The remembrances of those bright
happy Christmases at Windsor are constantly before me. None will ever be again what those
were, without you, dear Papa, and dear kind
Grandmama.

Darmstadt: December 27.

. . . I am sure you will have felt under many a
circumstance in life, that if any momentary feeling
was upon you, and you were writing to some one

near and dear, it did you good to put down those feelings on paper, and that, even in the act of doing so, when the words were barely written, the feeling had begun to die away, and the intercourse had done you good.

1868.

Darmstadt: January 24.

. . . To-night I am going to act with two other persons in our dining-room a pretty little piece called *Am Klavier*, but I fear I shall be very nervous, and consequently act badly, which would be too tiresome.

I have never tried to act in anything since *Rothkäppchen*.

February 1.

What a fright the news of dear Leopold's dangerous attack has given us! Mr. Sahl's letter to Becker arrived yesterday afternoon containing the bad news, and he spoke of so *little* hope, that I was so upset and so dreadfully distressed for the dear darling, for you, poor Mama, and for us all, that I am quite unwell still to-day.

When your telegram came to-day, and Louise's letter, I was so relieved and only pray and hope that the improvement may continue. May God

spare that young bright and gifted life, to be a
comfort and support to you for many a year to
come!

Had I only had a telegram! for, the letter being
two days old, until your telegram came I passed six
such agonising hours! Away from home, every news
of illness or sorrow there is so difficult to bear—
when one can share all the anxiety and trouble only
in thought.

The day passes so slowly without news, and I am
always looking towards the door to see if a telegram
is coming. Please let me hear regularly till he is
quite safe; I do love the dear boy, as I do all my
brothers and sisters, so tenderly!

How I wish you had been spared this new
anxiety! Those two days must have been dreadful!

Darling Mama, how I wish I were with you!
God grant that in future you may send us only
good news!

Louis and my parents-in-law send their respectful love and the expression of their warmest sympathy, in which the other members of the family
join.

February 2.

How glad and truly thankful I am, that the Almighty has saved our darling Leopold and spared

him to you and to us all! For the second or even
third time that life has been given again, when all
feared that it must leave us! A mother's heart must
feel this so much more than any other one's, and
dear Leopold, through having caused you all his
life so much anxiety, must be inexpressibly dear to
you, and such an object to watch over and take
care of. Indeed from the depth of my heart I
thank God with you for having so mercifully spared
dear Leo, and watched over him when death seemed
so near!

You will feel deeply now the great joy of seeing
a convalescence after the great danger, and I know,
through a thousand little things, how your loving
and considerate heart will find pleasure and consolation in cheering your patient.

That for the future you must ever be so anxious
is a dreadful trial, but it is to be hoped that Leo
will yet outgrow this strange illness. I am sure
good Archie* takes great care of him, and by this
time he will have gathered plenty of experience to
be a good nurse.

---

* Archibald Brown, his valet, younger brother of the
Queen's personal attendant.

Darmstadt: February 13.

. . . First let me wish you joy for the birth of this new grandson,* born on your dear wedding-day. I thought of you on the morning of the 10th, and meant to telegraph, but those dreadful neuralgic pains came on before I had time to look about me, and really laid me prostrate for the whole day, as they lasted so very long. I have never felt so un-well, or suffered so much in my life, and this mo-ment, sitting up in Louis' room, I feel more weak than I ever felt on first getting up after my con-finements. Quinine has kept me free from pain to-day, and I hope will do so to-morrow. I have been in bed a week and touched absolutely nothing all the time. Yesterday evening, as throughout the day, I had had (but much more slightly) a return of these agonising attacks, which seized my left eye, ear, and the whole left side of my head and nose. I got up and sat in Louis' room; I could only bear it for two hours, and all but fainted before I reached my bed. If I can get strength, and have no return of pain, I hope to go out after to-morrow. I could not see the children or anyone during this week,

* Prince Waldemar of Prussia, fourth son of the Crown Prince and Princess. He died of diphtheria on the 27th of March, 1879.

and always had my eyes closed, first from pain, and then from exhaustion when the pain left me. I really thought I should go out of my mind, and you know I can stand a tolerable amount of pain.

Darmstadt: February 24.

To my and, I fear, dear Vicky's great disappointment, Dr. Weber won't let me go to Berlin, and wants me to go to Wiesbaden for a cold-water cure instead. The latter will be intensely dull, as I shall be there for four weeks all alone; but I believe it will be very beneficial, as with every year I seem to get more rheumatic, which at my age is of course not good.

We shall hope to be able to come to Windsor, middle of June, as you desire. The exact time you will kindly let us know later.

Darmstadt: March 14.

I send you a few lines to-day for the 16th, the anniversary of the first great sorrow which broke in upon your happy life. How well do I recollect how I accompanied you and dear Papa down to Frogmore that night, our dinner in the flower room, the dreadful watching in the corridor, and then the so painful end! Darling Papa looked so pale, so deeply distressed, and was so full of tender sympathy for you. He told me to go to you and comfort you, and was so full of love and commiseration as I have never seen any man before or after. Dear, sweet Papa! that in that same year we should live together through such another heartrending scene again, and he not there to comfort or support you, poor Mama!

It sometimes, even at this distance of time, seems nearly impossible that we should have lived through such times, and yet be alive and resigned.

God's mercy is indeed great; for He sends a balm to soothe and heal the bruised and faithful heart, and to teach one to accommodate oneself to one's sorrow, so as to know how to bear it!

Darmstadt: April 5.

Only two words to-day, as my heart is so full of love and gratitude to you who took such care of me this day five years ago, who heard Victoria's first cry, and were such a comfort and help to us both. All these recollections make Victoria doubly dear to us, and, as in this world one never knows what will happen, I hope that you will always watch over our dear child, and let her be as dear to you as though she had been one of us.

April 3.

I am so distressed at dear, good Sir James
[Clark's] illness. I hope and trust that this precious
old friend will still be spared for a few years at
least.

Gotha: April 25.

. . . It is now eleven years since I spent my
birthday with dear Vicky, and she has been so
dear and kind, and dear Aunt and Uncle likewise.
We spend the day quite quietly together, and the
bad weather prevents any expeditions.

After to-morrow we go home.

Darmstadt: May 4.

Accept my best thanks for your last letter written
on dear Arthur's birthday. The playing of the band
I am sure gave him pleasure; but it would be too
painful for *all* ever to have it again on the terrace
as formerly. There are certain tunes, which that
Marine Band used to play, which, when I have
chanced to hear them elsewhere, have quite upset
me, so powerful does the recollection of those so
very happy birthdays at Osborne remain upon me!
Those happy, happy days touch me even to tears
when I think of them. What a joyous childhood

we had, and how greatly it was enhanced by dear, sweet Papa, and by all your great kindness to us!

I try to copy as much as lies in my power all these things for our children, that they may have an idea, when I speak to them of it, of what a happy home ours was.

I do feel so much for dear Beatrice and the other younger ones, who had so much less of it than we had!

Darmstadt: May 11.

For your sake I am sorry that my condition should cause you anxiety, for you have enough of that, God knows. But I am so well this time that I hope and trust all may go well, though one is never sure. It is this conviction which I always have, and which makes me serious and thoughtful, as who can know whether with the termination of this time my life may not also terminate?

This is also one of the reasons why I long so very much to see you, my own precious Mama, this summer, for I cling to you with a love and gratitude, the depth of which I know I can never find words or means to express. After a year's absence I wish so intensely to behold your dear, sweet, loving face again, and to press my lips on your dear hands. The older I grow the more I value and appreciate that mother's love which is unique in the world; and having, since darling Papa's death, only you, the love to my parents and to adored Papa's memory is all centred in *you*.

Louis has leave from the 11th of June to the 11th of August.

Uncle Ernest is coming here to-day for the day from Frankfort, where he has been to a cattle-show. Uncle Adalbert is here, so much pleased with having seen you again, singing the praise of both Lenchen and Louise, which of course I joined in, as it is such a pleasure to hear others admire and appreciate my dear sisters.

Darmstadt: May 14.

I know you will be grieved to hear that we all have had the grief of losing good, excellent Jäger.* He was, on the whole, better and was out daily, and he went to bed as usual, when in the middle of the night he called one of the men, and before they could come to his assistance he expired, having broken a blood-vessel. Poor Katrinchen's despair and grief were quite heartrending, when we went together to see our true and valued servant for the last time. I was so upset by the whole, that it was

---

* A footman, much valued by the Prince and Princess.

some days before I got over it. We made wreaths
to put on his coffin, which was covered with flowers
sent from all sides, and we both were at the door
with our servants when he was carried out, and
tried to console the poor unfortunate *Braut* [Bride],
who remained at home.

He was the best servant one could find; never,
since he has been in our service, had he been found
fault with by anyone. He was good, pious, and
gentle, and very intelligent. The death of a good
man, who has fulfilled his allotted duty in this
world as a good Christian ought, touches one
deeply, and we have really mourned for him as for
a friend, for he was one in the true sense of the
word. Jäger rests alongside my poor Willem, in
the pretty little cemetery here; a bit of my heart
went with them.

Fritz, on his way back from Italy, spent a few
hours with us, and told us much of his journey. He
heard the strangest rumours of France intending to
break out in sudden hostilities with Germany, and
asked me what you thought of a probability of a
war for this summer. I hope to God, that nothing
horrid of that sort will happen! Do you think it
likely, dear Mama?

Darmstadt: May 19.

My own darling and most precious Mama,

The warmest and tenderest wishes that grateful children can form for a beloved parent we both form for you, and these lines but weakly express all I would like to say. May God bless and watch over a life so precious and so dear to many! It is now six years since I spent that dear day near you, but I hope that some time or other we shall be allowed to do so. Our joint present is a medal for you with our heads. We had it made large in oxidised silver on purpose for you. I myself have braided and embroidered with Christa's help (who begged to be allowed to do something for you), a trimming for a dress, which I hope you will like and wear. It took a deal of my time, and my thoughts were so much with you while I was doing it, that I quite regretted its completion.

We are having a bracelet with our miniatures and the three children's in it made for you, but unfortunately it is not finished, so we shall bring it and give it to you ourselves.

Osborne: August 6.

I was just sitting down to write to you when Ernest came in with your dear letter. Thousand thanks for it! These parting lines will be such a

dear companion to me on our journey. I can't tell
you how much I felt taking leave of you this time,
dear Mama; it always is such a wrench to tear myself away from you and my home again. Where I
have so, oh, so much to be thankful and grateful
to you for, I always fear that I can never express
my thanks as warmly as I feel them, which I do
indeed from the bottom of my heart. God bless
you, darling Mama, for all your love and kindness;
and from the depth of my heart do I pray that nothing may cause you such anxiety and sorrow again
as you have had to bear of late. . . .

When I left you at the pier the return to the
empty house was so sad! It felt quite strange, and
by no means pleasant, to be here without you and
all the others. We lunched alone with Victoria,
and dined in the hot dining-room with the ladies
and gentlemen, sitting on the terrace afterwards.

It has rained all the morning, and is most op-
pressive. As it is so foggy, we have to leave at
two; but there is no wind, and I hope the sea will
be quite smooth. I am sure you must feel lonely
and depressed on this journey, poor Mama; but the
change of scene and beautiful nature enjoyed in
rest and quiet must surely do you good.

Kranichstein: August 10.

. . . We left Osborne at two on Thursday in rain and wind. The children and I were dreadfully sick an hour after starting, but the passage got smoother later: and, though I was very wretched in every way, I was not sick again. The same sort of weather on the *Alberta* next morning, but it cleared up later. The Rhine steamer was very comfortable, and Doctor Minter accompanied us to Dordrecht. The last afternoon and night on board I suffered dreadfully. Since I arrived here, I am better, but not right yet. Had it not been for your great kindness in giving us the ship, I am sure I should not have got home right. This awful heat adds to my feelings of fatigue and discomfort.

Kranichstein: August 11.

I have just received your letter from Lucerne, and hasten to thank you for it.

How glad I am that you admire the beautiful scenery, and that I know it, and can share your admiration and enjoyment of it in thought with you! It is most lovely. The splendid forms, and the colour of the lake, are two things that we don't know in dear Scotland, and which are so peculiar to Swiss scenery.

Louis is in town from eight till our two o'clock dinner, and has a great deal to do.

For your sake as for my own I long for a respite from this unbearable heat, which is so weakening and trying.

Kranichstein: August 16.

. . . How satisfactory the accounts of dear good Arthur are! From the depth of my heart do I congratulate you on all that Colonel Elphinstone says about his character, for with a real moral foundation, and a strict sense of duty and of what is right and wrong, he will have a power to combat the temptations of the world and those within himself. I am sure that he will grow up to be a pride and pleasure to you, and an honour to his country.

Brown must have been glad to be allowed to continue wearing his kilt, and, as it is a national dress, it is far more natural that he should give it up nowhere. I am sure that he and Annie* must admire the place.

Kranichstein: August 26.

I have just received your dear letter, and am so pleased to hear that you enjoyed your excursion,

---

* Mrs. McDonald, the Queen's first wardrobe-maid.

and that you have now seen the sort of wild scenery high up in the mountains, which I think so beautiful and grand in Switzerland. For all admirers of that style of scenery there is nothing to be compared to Switzerland.

Since it became cool again, I have had neuralgia in my head, and I have had a dreadful sty, which had to be cut open, and made me quite faint and sick for the whole day. In spite of it I went to the station here, with a thick veil on, to see the Russian relations pass two days ago. The Emperor looks even more altered and worn since last year, and is suddenly grown so old.

Kranichstein: September 4.

. . . How too delightful your expeditions must have been! I do rejoice that, through the change of weather, you should have been able to see and enjoy all that glorious scenery. Without your good ponies and Brown, &c., you would have felt how difficult such ascents are for common mortals, particularly when the horses slip, and finally sit down. I am sure all this will have done you good; seeing such totally new beautiful scenery does refresh so immensely, and the air and exertion—both of which you seem to bear so well now—will do your health good.

Yesterday we both were two hours at Jugenheim. To-day the two little cousins are coming to see my children.

Louis' business is increasing daily, and until the 19th, manœuvres, inspections, &c., won't be over. He will even have to be away on his birthday, which is a great bore. There is a great review for the Emperor on Saturday.

September 15.

. . . Like a foolish frightened creature as I am, I have worried myself so much about this sudden talk of war and threatening in all the French papers, saying that October, November, or thereabouts would be a good time to begin. Do tell me, if you think there is the least reasonable apprehension for anything of that sort this year. I have such confidence in your opinion, and you can imagine how in my present condition I must tremble before a recurrence of all I went through in 1866!

I am so grieved that you should have been so unwell on the journey home. Dear beautiful Scotland will do you good. I envy your going there, and wish I could be with you, for I am so fond of it. Remember me to all the good people.

Darmstadt: October 28.

. . . The Queen of Prussia is coming to lunch with us on Saturday on her way to Coblenz.

I have a cold these last days, and Victoria is still confined to the house with her swelled neck. She had quite lost her appetite, and I tried some porridge for her, which she enjoys, and I hope it will fatten her up a little, for she is so thin and pale. Would you please order a small barrel of oatmeal to be sent to me? Dr. Weber thinks it would be very good for Victoria, and one cannot get it here.

Darmstadt: November 20.

It is with the greatest interest that I read about the Mausoleum,* as I was very anxious to know whether all would be finished. Having been present before at all the important steps in the progress of this undertaking, I feel very sorry to be absent at the last, and I shall be very impatient to see it all again.

Winter has quite set in now here, and when there is no wind the cold is very pleasant.

Darmstadt: December 4.

Thousand thanks for all your dear kind wishes,

* The Royal Mausoleum at Frogmore.

for your first letter to me, for the one to Louis, and finally for the eatables! I can't tell you how touched, how pleased we both are at the kind interest all at home have shown us on this occasion. It has really enhanced our pleasure at the birth of our little son,* to receive so many marks of sympathy and attachment from those in my dear native home, and in my present one. My heart is indeed overflowing with gratitude for all God's blessings.

The time itself was very severe, but my recovery is up to now the best I have ever made, and I feel comparatively strong and well.

The girls are delighted with their brother though Victoria was sorry it was not a sister. Darling Louis was too overcome and taken up with me at first to be half pleased enough. Baby is to be called, by Louis' Uncle Louis' wish, *Ernst Ludwig*, after a former Landgrave**; then we would like you to give the name of *Albert; Charles*, after my father-in-law; and *William*, after the King of Prussia, whom we mean to ask to be godfather. The christening is most likely to be on the 28th or thereabout.

I am on my sofa in my sitting-room with all

* Hereditary Grand Duke Ernst Ludwig, born on the 28th November, 1868.

** Who died on the 8th of November, 1825.

your dear photos, &c., around me, and your pretty quilt over me.

December 12.

. . . Every new event in my life renews the grief for dear Papa's loss, and the deep regret that he was not here to know of all, to ask advice from, to share joy and grief with, for he was such a tender father, and would have been such a loving grandfather.

You, darling Mama, fill his place with your own, and may God's support never leave you and ever enable you to continue fulfilling the many duties towards State and family! The love of your children and people encircles you.

Darmstadt: December 18.

. . . The presents you intend giving Baby will delight us, and in later years I can tell him all about his Grandpapa, and how I wish and pray he may turn out in any way like him, and try and aim to become so.

I think it would be best, perhaps, if you asked my mother-in-law to represent you and hold Baby. I think it would pain her, should anyone else do it, and I will ask her in your name, if you will kindly telegraph to me your approval.

I am sorry Arthur cannot come; it would have given us such pleasure had it been possible.

The greater part of Baby's monthly gowns have been put away, as from the beginning they were too small. He is so very big.

Christmas Day.

. . . Louis thanks you a thousand times, as we do for the charming presents for the children. They showed them to everyone, shouting, "This is from my dear English Grandmama;" and Ella, who is always sentimental, added: "She is so very good, my Grandmama." Irène could not be parted from the doll you gave her, nor Victoria from hers. Baby was brought down, and was wide awake the whole time, looking about with his little bright eyes like a much older child.

We spent a very happy Christmas eve, surrounded by the dear children and our kind relations.

Darmstadt: December 29.

. . . Prince Hohenzollern with three gentlemen was sent by the King, and the former dined with us after the ceremony. All went off so well, and Baby, who is in every way like a child of two months, looked about him quite wisely, and was much admired by all who saw him.

I am so sorry that you have never seen my babies since Victoria, for I know you would admire them, they look so mottled and healthy. Weather permitting, Baby is to be photographed to-morrow.

1869.

. . . Dear charming Lady Frances [Baillie] is on a visit with us, and I enjoy having her so much. We talk of old times at Frogmore, and so many pleasant recollections.

I am glad that you like Baby's photograph, though it does not do him justice. He is a pretty baby on the whole, and has a beautiful skin, very large eyes, and pretty mouth and chin; but his nose is not very pretty, as it is so short at present. He is a dear good child, and, though immensely lively, does not give much trouble. He is a great source of happiness to us, and I trust will continue so.

. . . Is not the death of Leopold's son shocking?* Such suffering, such a struggle for months between

---

* The only son and heir of the King of the Belgians.

life and death; and for the poor parents to have in
the end to relinquish their child, their only son! I
think it heartrending. May the Almighty continue
to support them even now, as he did these many
months! I cannot say how much and truly I feel
for them both. This world is full of trials, and
some seem to be called upon to suffer and give up
so much. Faith and resignation alone can save
those hearts from breaking, when the burden must
be so heavy.

A few days ago at two o'clock we had another
shock [of earthquake], and it seemed as if the house
rocked; at the same time the unearthly noise. I
think it uncommonly unpleasant, particularly this
repetition.

                                                    January 30.

Our thoughts and prayers are so much with you
and dear Leopold on this day [his Confirmation].
May the Almighty bless and protect that precious
boy, and give him health and strength to continue
a life so well begun and so full of promise.

It seems to me quite incredible, the eighth of
us should already be old enough to take this step
in life, and to have his childhood in fact behind
him. Dear Papa's blessing surely rests on him, and
his spirit is near you as you stand there alone by

the side of his child, about whom he always was so anxious.

Darmstadt: March 8.

. . . We shall go to Potsdam the first week in May, and from there go for a week or ten days to Fischbach. My mother-in-law, Tante Mariechen,* and Uncle Adalbert** are all going to spend my mother-in-law's birthday there.

The Moriers are going to England in the first days of April, and I hope that you will see them. We see a good deal of them, and like them both much. He is wonderfully clever and learned, and takes interest in everything; and she is very agreeable, and a most satisfied, amiable disposition—always contented and amused.

March 19.

I thought of you so much on the 16th. From that day dated the commencement of so much grief and sorrow; yet in those days you had *one*, darling Mama, whose first and deepest thought was to comfort and help you, and I saw and understood only

* Queen of Bavaria, sister of Princess Charles of Hesse.
** Prince Adalbert of Prussia, brother of Princess Charles of Hesse.

then *how* he watched over you, and how and everywhere he sought to ward off all that was painful
and strange from you, and took all that pain alone
for himself, for your sake! I see his dear face—
so pale, and so full of tears, when he led me to you
early that morning after all was over, and said,
"Comfort Mama," as if those words were a *Vor-
bedeutung* [presage] of what was to come. In those
days, I think he knew how deep my love was for
you, and that, as long as I was left in my home, my
first and only thought should be you and you alone!
This I held as my holiest and dearest duty, until I
had to leave you, my beloved Mother, to form a
home and family for myself, and new ties which
were to take up much of my heart and strength.

But that bond of love, though I can no more be
near you, is as strong as ever.

Darmstadt: March 23.

. . . Yesterday it was very warm, and to-day it
snows; the weather continues so changeable, and
many people are ill. Ella has again had one of
her bad attacks in her throat, but, thank God, it
passed away very soon. Two nights ago she could
not speak—barely breathe—and was so uncomfort-
able, poor child! It makes one so anxious each

time; but I hope she will outgrow it, when she is six or seven years old.

Victoria is already now composing a letter for your birthday. I won't have her helped, because I should like you to see her own ideas and style—it is much more amusing.

March 26.

. . . We had such an unexpected pleasure the other day in the visit of good General Seymour, and I was so pleased to see some one who had seen you lately, and who could give me news of my home. He had not been here since he came with us after our marriage, and was of course interested in seeing everything.

April 2.

. . . The constant anxiety about the children is dreadful; and it is not physical ill one dreads for them, it is moral: the responsibility for these little lent souls is great, and, indeed, none can take it lightly who feel how great and important a parent's duty is.

Darmstadt: April 5.

. . . Thousand thanks for your dear letter, and for all the tender wishes for our dear child's birth-

day! The child born under your roof and your
care is of course your particular one, and later, if
you wish to keep her at any time when we have
been paying you a visit, we shall gladly leave her.

Victoria is so delighted with what you sent her,
and sends her very warmest thanks and her tenderest love. She is in great beauty just at present,
as she is grown stouter; and I look with pleasure
on those two girls when they go out together. They
possess, indeed, all we could wish, and are full of
promise. May the Almighty protect them and give
them a long life, to be of use and a joy to their
fellow-creatures!

April 16.

. . . Rain and wind have at length cooled the
air, for this heat without any shade was too unpleasant. Louis left at five this morning to inspect
the garrison at Friedberg and Giessen, and then to
go to Alsfeld to shoot *Auerhähne* [capercailzies].
He will return on the 21st or 22nd probably.

We shall indeed be so pleased, if later you wish
to have any of the granddaughters with you, to
comply with any such wish, for I often think so
sadly for your dear sake, how lonely it must be
when one child after another grows up and leaves
home; and even if they remain, to have no children

in the house is most dreary. Surely you can never lack to have some from amongst the many grand-children; and there are none of us, who would not gladly have our children live under the same roof where we passed such a happy childhood, with such a loving Grandmama to take care of them.

April 25.

. . . May I only know the way to give my chil-dren as much pleasure and happiness as you have ever known to give me!

The dinner of family and suite is here in the house to-day—or rather I should call it a luncheon, as it is at two o'clock.

The Irish Church question, I quite feel with you, will neither be solved nor settled in this way; and instead of doing something which would bring the Catholics more under the authority of the State, they will, I fear, be the more powerful. It seems to me that one injustice (with regard to the Protestants) is to be put in the place of a former one, instead of doing justice to both, which would not have been an impossibility through some well-considered settle-ment and giving in on both sides. Such a *change-ment* requires so much thought and wisdom, and, above all, impartiality.

4*

May 3.

. . . My children are, on the whole, very well
behaved and obedient, and, save by fits and starts,
which don't last long, very manageable.   I try to
be very just and consistent in all things towards
them, but it is sometimes a great trial of patience,
I own.   They are so forward, clever, and spirited,
that the least spoiling would do them great harm.

How glad I am that the dear Countess [Blücher]
is with you again! She is the pleasantest companion
possible, and so dear and loving, and she is devoted
to you and dear Papa's memory as never anyone
was.

Potsdam: May 25.

How much we thought of you yesterday, I can't
say.   Lord Augustus Loftus lunched with us three
and the elder children; and we drank your health,
the band playing "God save the Queen!"   All our
girls had wreaths of natural flowers in honour of
the day.

Potsdam: June 1.

. . . To-day is regular March weather, and the
palace is cold and draughty.

We were in Berlin yesterday, to visit the Ge-
werbe-Museum [Industrial Museum]; then luncheon

at Lord Augustus Loftus's, and from thence to the Victoria bazaar and Victoria Stift, and then home.

It is always so tiring to see things at Berlin; an hour's rail there and the same back takes so much time. Before returning, we paid a short visit to Baron Stockmar and his wife, who is very pleasing, and seems to suit him perfectly. They look as if they had always belonged to each other.

Potsdam: June 13.

Our time here is soon drawing to a close, much to my regret; for the life with dear Vicky—so quiet and pleasant—reminds me in many things of our life in England in former happy days, and so much that we had Vicky has copied for the children. Yet we both always say to each other, no children were so happy, and so spoiled with all the enjoyments and comforts children can wish for, as we were; and that we can never (of course, still less I) give our children all that we had. I am sure dear Papa and you, if you could ever hear how often, how tenderly, Vicky and I talk of our most beloved parents, and how grateful we are for what they did for us, would in some measure feel repaid for all the trouble we gave, and all the anxiety we caused. I ever look back to my childhood and girlhood as the happiest time of my life. The responsibilities, and often the want of many a thing, in married life can never give unalloyed happiness.

We are looking for a governess for the two elder girls for next year, and a lady with the necessary knowledge and character, and yet of a certain rank, is so difficult to find.

Potsdam: June 19.

Louis went two days ago to Fischbach for his mother's birthday, and returns to-morrow morning. Vicky was very low yesterday; she has been so for the last week, and she told me much of what an awful time she went through in 1866, when dear Siggie [Sigismund] died. The little chapel is very peaceful and cheerful, and full of flowers. We go there *en passant* nearly daily, and it seems to give dear Vicky pleasure to go there.

Vicky goes on the 7th of July to Norderney.

Fischbach, Schlesien: July 2.

We arrived here in this exquisitely lovely country two days ago, and were received by our parents-in-law and Aunt Mariechen, whose guests we are in the pretty old Castle of Fischbach, sourrounded by fine old trees, with a view on the beautiful Riesengebirge, which reminds me a little of Scotland, and also of Switzerland. The valleys are most lovely, and the numberless wooded hills, before one reaches the high mountains, are quite beautiful. The trees are splendid, and the country looks very rich and green.

All the people of the village and the neighbourhood came out to see us and our children, and old servants of Louis' grandparents, who were so delighted and pleased that I and my children should be here, and that they should have lived to see the younger generation.

We are out seeing the beautiful spots nearly all day long. The weather is fine, and not very warm, so that one can go about comfortably. Yesterday we went over for tea to Erdmannsdorf. If only dear Vicky and Fritz were there now! We must hope for another year to be there together. The parting from them, who had made our *séjour* under their hospitable roof such a very happy one, was very sad, and the pouring rain was in accordance with our feelings. We left them and dear lovely Potsdam and the pleasant life there with much regret, and many a blessing do I send back in thought to its dear inmates.

Yesterday afternoon we were at Schmiedeberg. We went to see a very interesting carpet-manufactory, worked by hand, and all by girls, and a very simple process, much like making fringe, which you used to do and then make footstools of after Beatrice's birth.

Yesterday our wedding-day—already seven years ago—made me think so much of Osborne, and of you, darling Mama, and of all that passed during that time. It was a quiet wedding in a time of much sorrow, and I often think how trying it must have been for you.

Kranichstein: July 21.

Yesterday, after eighteen hours' very hot railway journey, we arrived here all well. Many thanks for your letter, which I received at Dresden. It was impossible to write, as I had to pay visits and to see things, during those two days.

I went to see the picture-gallery, which has some exquisite pictures, though the Sistine Madonna surpasses all others, and the famous Holbein, of which the Dresden gallery has been for long so proud, is now recognised as a copy, and the one that belongs to my mother-in-law as the original. We visited the Grüne Gewölbe [the Green Vaults], where the magnificent jewels and other treasures are preserved, and the King was kind enough to lead us over the rest of the castle himself, including his own rooms, in one of which the life-size pictures of his last four daughters (all dead) stand, of whom he cannot speak without tears. How dreadfully he and the poor Queen must have suffered these last years!

Kranichstein: July 25.

Thousand thanks for your kind letter which I received yesterday, at the same time that the beautiful christening present for Ernest arrived! Thousand thanks for this most beautiful and precious gift for our boy, from Louis and from myself! We are so pleased with it! It is to be exhibited here, and it will interest and delight all who see it, I am sure.

I have just received a letter from Bertie, announcing his arrival here for the 28th. We shall be greatly pleased to see them all; but we have so little room, and our house in town is all shut up and under repair, so that we shall have some trouble to make them comfortable and shall be quite unable to do it as we should wish. But I trust they will be lenient and put up with what we can offer.

The heat is very great, though this place is comparatively cool.

Kranichstein: August 11.

. . . Victoria has often ridden on Dred, and also the other girls, on a Spanish saddle, and he goes very well. They delight in him. Baby rolls about

the room anywhere now, and tries to crawl properly.
He calls Papa, and tries no end of things; he is
very forward, and is now cutting his fifth tooth,
which is all but through.

Friedberg: August 26.

On this dear day I must send you a few words.
The weather is so beautiful, and the sun so bright,
as it used to be at Osborne in former years. I don't
care for the sun to shine on this day now, as it can't
shine on Him whose day it was. It makes one too
wehmüthig to think of darling Papa on those happy
birthdays, and it must be more so for you than for
any of us, poor Mama.

Yesterday was Ludwigstag; all the town decorated with flags, illuminations, &c., and English
flags and arms with the Hessian everywhere.

We started on horseback along the high road at
half-past seven this morning, and did not get off till
one. A lovely country and very interesting to see.
To-morrow we shall have a very long march, and
the night Alice Morier,* I and William (Louis is undecided) will spend at Prince Ysenburg's at Büdingen.
The next morning we have to ride off at half-past
five; and a long day back here.

* Mrs. now Lady Morier, daughter of General Peel.

Kranichstein: September 11.

. . . What charming expeditions you must have made in that lovely country!* What I saw of it some years ago I admired so intensely. You can well be proud of all the beauties of the Highlands, which have so entirely their own stamp, that no Alpine scenery, however grand, can lessen one's appreciation for that of Scotland.

The day before yesterday we went to Mayence to see a "Gewerbe-Ausstellung" [Industrial Exhibition] of the town, which was very good and tastefully arranged. From there we went to Frankfort to our palace, for a rendezvous with Aunt Cambridge, Uncle George, Augusta and Fritz Strelitz. I showed them the children, and afterwards, when our relations left, we took our children to the Zoological Garden, which delighted them.

Many thanks for the grouse, which has just arrived, the first since two years ago!

Darmstadt: October 3.

. . . I am very glad that you also approve of Louis' journey, which I know will be so useful and

---

* This refers to the Queen's stay at Invertrossachs, and the excursions to the neighbourhood. These are described in *More Leaves from a Journal of a Life in the Highlands*, pp. 99-121.

interesting for him, though it was not possible to
attain this without parting from each other, which
is, of course, no small trial for us, who are so unac-
customed to being separated. But we never thought
of that when we considered the plan of Louis join-
ing Fritz, which was my idea, and travelling in new
countries is so good for a man, and Louis may never
find so good a chance again. I am looking forward
very much to seeing Geneva—where we spend a day
—and the south of France, and, above all, seeing
the sea again. Fritz passes through here to-morrow.
Louis starts Saturday morning, *viâ* Munich, for
Venice, where he will join Fritz next Sunday afternoon, and spend the following Monday there before
they go to Brindisi. Vicky comes here with her
children on the 12th or 13th, and a suite of twenty-
five people. She goes on with the big boys to
Baden, and I follow with the other children on the
following day. I don't like separating Victoria and
Ella, who like being together; the three girls will be
so well taken care of at their grandparents'. I have
written down rules for meals, going out, to bed, to
lessons, &c.; and my mother-in-law, who never inter-
feres, will see that all is carried out as I wish. I
shall miss them so much, but having one child at
least is a comfort; and Baby is beginning to talk,
and is so funny and dear, and so fond of me, that

he will be company to me when I am alone. I take no one but Orchard, Eliza, Beck, and my Haus-hofmeister [steward], who used to be with Lord Granville.

          Darmstadt: October 11.

 Yesterday morning at eleven we had the hard separation from each other, which we both felt very much. My own dear, tender-hearted Louis was quite in the state he was in when we parted at Windsor in 1860 after our engagement. He does not like leaving his children, his home, and me, and really there are but few such husbands and fathers as he. To possess a heart like his, and to call it my *own*, I am ever prouder of and more grateful for from year to year. Nowadays young men like Louis are rare enough, for it is considered fine to neglect one's wife, and for the wife also to have amusements in which her husband does not share. We sisters are singularly blessed in our husbands.

 Dear kind Countess Blücher has been here the last two days—such a happiness to me just now, for the house feels far too lonely.

       Grand Hôtel, Cannes: November 5.

 . . . I have this instant received another letter from dear Louis from Constantinople, giving the

accounts of what they did and saw there until the
29th ult., when they left for Jaffa. He seems delighted, and very greatly interested with all he has
seen. Louis thought so much of the Sultan's
English visit in 1867, on seeing him again. He
found him more talkative than then. He saw also
several of the suite who were in England. They
went to Scutari, into the Black Sea, and visited all
in and near Constantinople, and on the last day
they visited the Emperor of Austria, who had just
arrived. There is something very funny in hearing
of these Royalties, one after another, all running to
the same places. They must bore the Sultan con-
siderably.

This journey will be of great advantage to dear
Louis, who has never had an opportunity (through
marrying so young) of travelling like others.

This afternoon we went to see poor Princess
Waldeck. * She is still in great grief at the loss of
her eldest daughter, who suffered so long, and knew
she was dying, and bore her lot with such resignation and such goodness. She was only fifteen-and-
a-half, I think.

I was very much pleased to see Lord and Lady
Russell again the other day. We hope to be able

---

* Mother of the Duchess of Albany.

to pay them a visit at San Remo, though one can't go and return in the same day.

The country has looked too lovely to-day; the sunset is always most beautiful, for it sets behind the Esterel mountains, which lie to the right from this bay, and have a very lovely jagged form.

I am reading to Vicky a new Life of Napoleon, by Lanfrey, which is very well and impartially written.

Cannes: December 14.

. . . The heavenly blue sea, stretching so far and wide, is in accordance with one's feelings, and the beauties of nature have always something comforting and soothing. . . .

The Duke of Argyll's sister, with his pretty daughter Victoria, are here, and we have been twice to see them, and are distressed that they should be so anxious about the dear Duchess, of whom the news to-day is worse. How dreadful, should anything happen to her, for her husband and for the many children!

The Elburys and Lord Dalhousie have likewise arrived here, but we have not seen them yet.

To-morrow we had intended leaving this, but during the night poor Vicky had the dreadful fright

of Waldie's being taken ill with the croup. Thank
God, he is better this morning, but our journey
will have to be put off for a few days, so that
Vicky cannot now reach Berlin in time for Christmas. As we don't wish to spend that day *en route*,
we have telegraphed to our husbands, who reach
Naples to-day, to ask whether they will not join us
here, that we may all spend Christmas together before leaving.

This is all unsettled, and I will telegraph as
soon as anything is definitively arranged. Rollet *
is here to-day, and spends this day in quiet
with us.

Cannes: December 20.

We both had the happiness yesterday of receiving our dear husbands safe and well here after
so long a separation.

They had been to Naples and Pompeii, and
Louis went for a day to Rome, so that he has seen
an enormous deal, which is very instructive for
him, and will be such a pleasure for him to look
back upon in later years.

I am so glad that Louis has had the opportunity

* Madame Rollande, formerly the Princess's French governess.

of making this journey; and it seems to have done
his health good also, for he looks very well.

The journey back is so long and difficult for
me to manage alone with Louis—as Vicky's people,
particularly in the nursery, have helped mine—
that I am obliged to wait until the 26th, and to
go with Vicky and Fritz, for they travel slower
than I would do if I went with Louis, who goes
back direct day and night. The doctor would not
consent to my travelling with Ernie from this
warm climate into the great cold so fast, and during
the night, for he is cutting four back teeth at this
moment.

The day before yesterday we visited Lord Dalhousie and Lady Christian, and found him very
gouty, but in good spirits. Lady Ebury and Oggie *
came to see us this afternoon. Prince and Princess
Frederic of the Netherlands and their daughter
have arrived here. The poor Princess is so weak,
and looks like a shadow.

Hôtel du Jura, Dijon: December 28.

Just as we were leaving Cannes your last letter
reached me, for which many thanks. It was cold
the morning we left Cannes, very cold at Avignon,

* Miss Grosvenor, Lady Ebury's daughter.

where we spent the night, and still colder, and
snow and frost, on reaching this place yesterday
evening. We and the children are all well, and
the poor little ones are very good on the journey,
considering all things. In an hour we leave for
Paris, rest there to-morrow, and then go to Cologne,
where I shall take leave of dear Vicky and Fritz,
and go straight home. I have been so much
with dear Vicky this year, that the thought of
parting from her costs me a great pang, the more
so as I do not think it likely that I shall meet her
in this new year.

On New Year's eve I arrange a Christmas-tree
for all my children, and in advance I thank you
for all the presents you have been kind enough
to send us, and which we shall find at Darmstadt. . . .

1870.

January 8.

. . . My three girls have had fearful colds— Ella bronchitis, which Ernie also took from her, and during twelve hours we were in the very greatest anxiety about him: the difficulty of breathing and his whole state caused great alarm. Thank God, he is now quite convalescent; but those were hours of intense suffering for me, as you can imagine. Weber is most attentive and most kind on such occasions, and in such moments one is so dependent on the doctor.

. . . Some very good lectures have been given here lately, undertaken by a committee, which we are at the head of, and of which Mr. Morier is a member. They have been a great success hitherto, and we are going to one to-night by Kinkel, who in 1848 was a refugee in England, and is now a professor at Zürich.

January 16.

Beloved Mama,

We are very grateful for your kind inquiries, and for your letter received this morning. The violence of the fever and the great pain in the throat have abated, and dear Louis is going on favourably.* The nights are not good as yet, and his head pains him.

I am cut off from all intercourse with anyone in the house, on account of the dear children; and I trust they may escape, for they still cough, particularly Ella and Ernie. I see Christa when I am out walking, not otherwise, as she comes in contact with the part of the house where the children live. I read to Louis, and play to him, as my sitting-room opens into the bedroom. I keep the rooms well aired, and not hot, and at night I sleep on a sofa near his bed. The first two nights were anxious ones, and I was up all night alone with him; but now, thank God, all seems to be going well. . . .

January 20.

I am happy to say that all is going on well. Louis has no more fever, but his throat is still far

---

* Prince Louis was ill with an attack of scarlet fever.

from well; it has still the character of diphtheria, though in a mild form—a sort of skin and bits of blood come away when he coughs. He is a very good patient, and I leave him very little alone save when I take my walks, which in this high cold wind are very unpleasant. I hear Ella is still so hoarse and coughs, and Victoria is not quite well. Orchard writes to me every evening, and Dr. Weber * sees them in the morning before he comes downstairs.

This instant Weber tells me that Victoria has the scarlet fever, and I have just been up to see her. She suffers very much, poor child; the fever is very high and the rash much out. It is too late now to separate the others, and those who are not predisposed will escape; but those who are inclined to take it have it in them by this time.

It is a source of great anxiety. Orchard and Emma have never had it. . . .

January 23.

I was very glad to get your dear lines of the 22nd, full of sympathy for me during this anxious time. Victoria's fever has been very high; and so much discomfort and pain, with a dreadful cough,

* Prince and Princess Louis' own physician.

which she has had for the last six weeks. She is very low, and cries every now and then from weakness, &c., but is a very good patient, poor little one! Amelung comes every afternoon and sits with her, and she is a great favourite with the children, as she knows countless pretty stories.

Louis is not out of bed yet, on account of his throat, &c.; but he is much better, though in this treacherous climate, which is proverbially bad for throats and lungs, I fear that even with the greatest care there is a risk.

The other children are as yet well, though I don't think Ella looking well; she has still a cold, and is as hoarse as when I came home. Ernie is all right again, and looks the best of them all. I doubt their escaping, though it is quite possible, as they did not take it when Victoria did. I keep the rooms fresh, and continually aired.

All the balls and parties are going on here now. Of course, I can neither go anywhere nor receive anyone, on account of the infection. It is a wearisome time indeed, and being so much in sick rooms and so little out begins to tell upon me. How kind of you to send the books! Louis will be delighted. I have just read to him Russell's book of Bertie and Alix's journey, and am now reading to him a new Life of Napoleon, by Lanfrey, which is

very well written—more against than for Napoleon.
Of course, newspapers and the *Revue des Deux-
Mondes* I read to him besides. . . .

January 31.

. . . Though dear Baby has had two bad, rest-
less nights, yet I am happy to say that he has the
illness so slightly, with so little fever or sore throat,
that we are in great hopes it will get no worse. He
is cutting his back teeth just now, which is the worst
moment possible to be ill in.

Victoria looks very hollow-eyed, pale and
wretched, poor darling, but is in good spirits now.
The other two are as yet free. The weather is most
beautiful—frosty and clear—and I have been skat-
ing daily for the last six days, which does me much
good, and enables me to see people again. This
afternoon I have a large party on the ice at Kranichstein, and this is always a great amusement to the
young people. . . .

Mayence: April 10.

. . . Yesterday evening we had to give a large
party here, half to the military, and the other to the
civil authorities and to the *Bürger* [citizens]. It
went off well; but the amount of speaking, as one
must speak to all, and the effort to remember who

they all were—they having been all presented at once—was no small exertion. . . .

Mayence: April 15.

. . . Lady Car. [Barrington] wrote to me how very grateful Mrs. Grey was to you for your great kindness and consideration.* In trouble no one can have a more true and sympathising friend than my beloved Mama always is. How many hearts has she not gained by this, and how many a poor sufferer's burdens has she not lightened! . . .

April 25.

Thousand thanks for your dear loving lines! I kissed them a thousand times, and thank you so much for the quite lovely statuette—a little gem, which everyone has been admiring this morning. The shawl and little ornament gave me also great pleasure, and the coloured photographs of the rooms —in short, all and anything from such dear hands must give pleasure. . . .

June 25.

. . . I am proud of my two girls, for they are warm-hearted and gifted, too, in appearance. Victoria's

---

* General Grey, Her Majesty's private secretary, who died March 30.

facility in learning is wonderful, and her lessons are her delight. Her English history and reading she has learned from me. I give her a lesson daily, and Bäuerlein* can tell you how much she has learned. . . .

I read a great deal, chiefly history and deeper works; and I have one or two very learned acquaintances with whom to read or to have books recommended by.

My two committees always give me no end of work, and I have tried to have many improvements made in the girls' schools of the different classes; and some of these things, by dint of a deal of trouble, are prospering, and I hope in time to come will prove their worth. There is a great deal to be done, and in the hospitals I have been able to get some very necessary changes made. I tell you all this, fancying it may perhaps interest you a little bit. . . .

July 2.

How grieved I am for your sake, above all, and for the poor Clarks and ourselves, that dear kind Sir James,** that true fatherly friend, is no more!!

---

* Miss Bauer, the German governess of the Royal family.
** Sir James Clark died at Bagshot June 29, 1870.

Many thanks for your last letter, which tells me of your last visit to him, which I am sure must be a great comfort to you. Oh! how sad to think how many are gone! And for you, dear Mama, this is quite dreadful. I can't say how I feel it for you!

Lord Clarendon's death* grieves me much also; and it was so sudden. Alice Skelmersdale wrote to me in the greatest distress; he had been a most loving father.

In the midst of life we are in death; and in our quiet and solitary existence out here, where we see no one, all accords with sad and serious feelings, which, amidst the many people and worry you live in, must jar with such feelings and make you wish for solitude. The accounts you give touch me so much. Many thanks for having written so much about dear Sir James; it is of great value to me. Louis begs me to say how he shares the grief you all and we must feel at such a loss.

What you say about the education of our girls I entirely agree with, and I strive to bring them up totally free from pride of their position, which is *nothing*, save what their personal worth can make it. I read it to the governess—who quite enters into all my wishes on that subject—thinking how

* Died June 27, 1870.

good it would be for her to hear your opinion. . . .
I feel so entirely as you do on the difference of
rank, and how all-important it is for princes and
princesses to know that they are nothing better or
above others, save through their own merit; and
that they have only the double duty of living for
others and of being an example—good and modest.
This I hope my children will grow up to.

July 26.

When I returned home last night really heartbroken, after having parted from my good and
tenderly loved Louis, I found your dear sympathising words, and I thank you a thousand times for
them—they were a comfort and pleasure to me!
I parted with dear Louis late in the evening, on the
high road outside the village in which he was
quartered for the night, and we looked back until
nothing more was to be seen of each other. May
the Almighty watch over his precious life, and bring
him safe back again! All the pain and anxiety are
forgotten and willingly borne if he is only left to
me and to his children!

It is an awful time, and the provocation of a
war such as this a crime that will have to be an-
swered for, and for which there can be no justifica-
tion. Everywhere troops and peasants are heard

singing "Die Wacht am Rhein" and "Was ist des Deutschen Vaterland?" and there is a feeling of unity and standing by each other, forgetting all party quarrels, which makes one proud of the name of German. All women feel ashamed of complaining, when father, husband, or son goes, and so many as volunteers in the ranks. This war is felt to be national, and that the King had no other course left him to pursue with honour.

I must be in town by nine o'clock: so much rests on me, and there are so many to help—the poor forsaken soldiers' families amongst others! I have seen that all is ready to receive the wounded, and to send out help. I send out fourteen nurses for the Feld-Lazarethe [field-hospitals].

How much I feel for you now, for I know how truly you must feel for Germany; and *all* know that every good thing England does for Germany, and every evil she wards off her, is owing to your wisdom and experience, and to your true and just feelings. You would, I am sure, be pleased to hear how universally this is recognised and appreciated.

What would beloved Papa have thought of this war? The unity of Germany, which it has brought about, would please him, but never the shocking means!

July 28.

My darling Louis is at Worms, and Henry just in front of him. The enthusiasm all along the Rhine is wonderful. They are all hopeful, though knowing well what enormous sacrifices and struggles a victory will cost.

I cannot leave this place until our troops should have—which God prevent!—to retreat, and the French come! Now is the moment when a panic might overcome the people; and I think it my duty to remain at my post, as it gives the people courage and confidence. My parents-in-law, who have their three sons out, would feel my absence, and they have the first claim on me. I am in beloved Louis' home, and nearer to him, if I remain. Of course, with dear Vicky I should personally be far better off. But Fritz is not much exposed, and she has not that fearful anxiety to such an amount as I have for dear Louis, who, as commander of only a division, must be in the very midst of all. Day and night this thought is uppermost in my mind. I hope and pray for the best, and bear what is sent to me in common with so many others. Work is a *Zerstreuung* [distraction], and I know dear Louis would prefer knowing me here for the present, and that must be the first consideration to determine my actions.

Louis is well, and, now the dreadful parting is over, I am sure in better spirits, though work and anxiety weigh on him, poor love.

The children send their love. I am pretty well; able to do a great deal; headache and sleeplessness are but natural at this moment.

August 5.

Arrived in our house this morning, I was received with the news of dear Fritz's first victory,* and that 500 French prisoners had just passed through here by rail. I know none of ours can have been engaged, but we have not heard if there was an engagement elsewhere. The excitement and anxiety are quite dreadful! Please God, my darling is safe, and will pass safely through these dreadful dangers —and our many dear friends and acquaintances also! I am always sending off things for the wounded from our stores, and continue working and collecting, and all are most patriotic and united. It is a solemn and great time we live in, and there is something grand and elevating in the unity of high and low throughout this great nation, which makes one proud of belonging to it. If only all goes on well!

* Victory of the Germans at Weissenburg over Marshal MacMahon, on August 4, 1870.

I am very sleepless, and never without headache,
but one has neither time nor wish to think of oneself. My own Louis' safety is the all-engrossing
thought; and I know, beloved Mama, that you love
him truly, and share this anxiety with me. . . .

August 15.

A few words by messenger. I have sent a letter
by Kanné,* who came here yesterday, having seen
dear Louis the day before, which was the first
direct news I have had from him. Yesterday morning he was at Faulquemont. Poor General von
Manstein (our Chef), when he reached Saarbrück,
found his son had been killed, and he had him
taken out of the general grave and buried in the
churchyard. . . . No less than forty French wounded
I saw this morning in our hospital, with some Turcos.
Some can't speak in any known language, and the
French dislike having these savages near them as
much as we do; their physiognomies are horrid,
and they steal and murder as *Handwerk* [their
vocation].

So much going about—for I go to Darmstadt
at half-past eight, and remain till half-past eleven,
in the morning, and in the afternoon from five till

---

* The Queen's own courier.

eight—is getting very fatiguing to me; but the people have no time to come out here, and there is much to see to, and many to speak with.

August 19.

I have tried to write as often as I could, but I have only two hours to myself during the whole day, through driving in here twice a day. Besides the large Hülfsverein for the "wounded and sick," which is in our palace, I have daily to visit the four hospitals. There is very much to do; we are so near the seat of war. This morning we got two large waggons ready and sent off for Pont-à-Mousson, where they telegraph from the battlefield of the 16th they are in great want. My best nurses are out there; the others are in three hospitals: two of them—military ones—were not ready or organised when 150 wounded arrived a week ago. I have just had a telegram from dear Louis; he is well, and I hope in a day or two the least dangerously of the Hessian wounded will arrive.

Thank God, all goes on successfully; but, indeed, I hope I shall not live to see another such war—it is too shocking by far. We have over five hundred wounded; as soon as any are better, they are sent north, and worse ones fill the beds—French and German intermixed. I neither see nor smell anything else but wounds! and the first *Anblick* [sight], which sometimes one does not escape meeting, is very shocking! It was very late last night before I got home. I was stopped at one of the hospitals, as a poor soldier had had sudden violent bleeding, and was all but dead, as the doctor could not find the artery; but I sent my carriage for another surgeon, and I am happy to say he lives, and is recovering.

As Louis commands the whole of our little army, a great many things concerning the troops come to me from all parts of the country, and there is much to do—much more than in my present state is good for me; but it can't be helped.

I drive back to Kranichstein by one daily, and am here again before five, so I hope you will kindly forgive my writing seldomer. Becker is engrossed with his duties at the Hülfsverein; there is no other gentleman with me, and I have the household to look after, besides.

August 20.

My telegram will have told you that dear Louis is until now safe.* On the 16th, in the evening,

---

* On the 16th, Marshal Bazaine, while retreating from Metz to Verdun, was attacked by Prince Frederic Charles, be-

and on the 17th and 18th, our troops were engaged,
and yesterday evening late I drove to the station,
to speak to General Kehrer, our commandant, and
received a telegram of the last victory, near Metz—
a battle of nine hours, very bloody—no mention of
names. The people, all excited, crowded round
my carriage, asked for news—which of our regiments had been under fire? I could tell them nothing, but pacified them, begging them to go to
their homes—they should hear as soon as I had
news. I drove home with an aching heart, and
passed a dreadful night of suspense. At six this
morning a telegram from Louis (19th); he and his
two brothers safe; our loss enormous—seventy
officers out of one division (ours is the 25th), and
Oberlieutenant Möller, a great favourite, his adjutant
since 1866, very badly wounded. I went at once
to Darmstadt to Louis' parents. They were so overcome and thankful to hear of the safety of their
children. This continual anxiety is fearful. Now
to-day all the poor wives, mothers, sisters, come to
me for news of their relations; it is heartrending!

tween Vionville and Mars-la-Tour, and a severe engagement
was fought. On the 17th and 18th occurred the battles of Re-
zonville and Gravelotte, in which the King of Prussia com-
manded, and defeated Marshal Bazaine. Prince Louis was engaged with his division in these battles.

We sent off two large waggon-loads to Pont-à-
Mousson again with provisions, bandages and
medicaments, and mattresses to bring back all the
wounded possible by rail. I went the round of the
hospital, to have all the convalescent Prussians and
French able to travel sent to their homes, so as to
get room, and now we can await the sad arrivals.
Oh, if it would but end! the misery of thousands is
too awful!

Kranichstein: August 25.

Many thanks for your dear words of the 20th.
God knows, I have suffered much, and the load of
anxiety is great! But thousands of Germans bear
this load in unity together for their Fatherland, and
none murmur. Yesterday a poor woman came to
me to ask me to help her to get to the battlefield,
to have the body of her only son looked for and
brought home; and she was so resigned and patient.

I see daily, in all classes, so much grief and
suffering; so many acquaintances and friends have
fallen! It is heartrending! I ought to be *very proud*
though, and I am so, too, to hear from the mouths
of so many wounded officers the loud praise of
Louis' great bravery on the 16th and 18th. Always
in front, encouraging his men where the battle raged

6*

fiercest and the balls fell thickest. He was near our troops, speaking to them, directing them, and right and left of him they fell in masses. This lasted eight hours!

. . . Hourly almost the trains bring in fresh wounded, and many and shocking are the sights one sees. I only returned here by one, having gone to town at half-past eight this morning, and have still three hospitals for this afternoon.

My nurses reached the battlefield in time, and were of great use. Louis telegraphed (yesterday's date) from Auboué, between Thionville and Metz, where they remain in bivouac. . . . It is ten days since Louis has been in a bed or under a roof. They have no water (it is kept for the wounded), and little to eat, but he is very well.

It is difficult to get news, and I can never send any that is not mostly ten days old ere it reaches him.

August 26.

. . . I had a telegram on the 25th from near Marengo, not far from Metz—all well. Louis has not been in bed or under a roof since the 16th, and it rains incessantly. I hope they won't all be ill. He writes mostly on cards, on the hilt of his sword, sitting on a box. They cook their own dinner, and

on the 16th they were going to eat it, when orders
came to turn the French left wing and go into
battle. That night was awful, though the day of
the 18th seems to have been the bloodiest ever
known. Our wounded all tell me so.

My dear parents-in-law bear up well; but when
we three get together we pour our hearts out to
each other, and then tears which are full of anxiety
will flow.

Kranichstein: September 2.

I went early to Homburg, as no trains go regularly. I went by road from Frankfort, and found
dear Vicky well—her little baby very pretty and
healthy-looking; the other dear children also well.

How much we had to tell each other! How much
to be proud of, and how many friends and acquaintances to mourn over! The few hours we had together flew by in no time, and at Frankfort the train
was unpunctual—outside Darmstadt it waited nearly
an hour. At our palace, where I arrived at ten in
the evening, people who were going to our Haupt-
quartier [headquarters] were waiting. I scribbled a
few words to my dear Louis (the first since he received the Iron Cross, a great distinction) and packed
a few things for him—tea, &c.

September 15.

Though I am still forbidden to use my eyes, I must send you a few words of thanks for your dear letter and telegram. I had a violent inflammation of eyes and throat, with two days strong fever and neuralgia. I am recovering now, but feel the effects very much; my eyes are still bad, and it has reduced my strength, which I require so much. Dr. Weber has just lost his sister (whom he treated in her confinement) from puerperal fever, and he told me he thought he must have given it to her, from going to and fro to his wounded, for *Lazarethfieber* [hospital fever] and that were so closely akin. You can fancy that in Louis' absence, and with the prospect of being alone, without even a married experienced lady in the house, this prospect frightened me. It is unhealthy at any time to be for one's confinement in a town full of hospitals with wounded, and Weber could never give me as much attention as at another time, and, should I be very ill, there is no authority to say anything about what had best be done. On that account your telegram was a relief to me.

September 20.

. . . Daily I hear the muffled drums of the funeral of some soldier or officer being taken past my windows to his last resting-place. How deeply I do feel for the poor parents and widows!

My children are very well, but have absolutely no place where they can walk with safety from infection, for the mass of sick troops who get out and stop near the Exercirplatz [drill-ground], and the hospitals in town. The barrack at the foot of our garden contains 1,200 French prisoners, and many of them ill. It is much to be hoped that there will be soon an end to all these things. I feel for the Emperor and Empress very much. What ungrateful, vain, and untruthful people the French are! To expose Paris to a siege, now their armies are beaten, which they think through fine speeches and volunteers they can set right again.

September 22.

I received your letter through Kanné yesterday, and thank you many times for it; also for the little shawls and sash for Ernie. Every souvenir from dear Balmoral is a pleasure.

Good Dr. Hofmeister* will be very welcome, and I know he is very clever. Mrs. Clarke** is sure to

---

* Sent by the Queen to attend the Princess in her confinement.

** Nurse.

get on well with him, and an older doctor just now, besides being an acquaintance of so many years, is to me indeed a comfort. I shall be able also to hear of all at home, and of so many things that interest me. Thousand thanks from Louis and from myself for your sending him! . . .

ALL long for peace—the army and the nation— and I think so great a national war as this need not require part of the foes' territory. What little is necessary for the military frontier they must take; but the union of Germany under one head is a far greater and finer end to such a war than the annexation of land!

. . . War is the greatest scourge this world knows, and that we may not live to see it again, is my earnest prayer.

October 1.

. . . The children are all well, in spite of the bad air here. I send them out driving of an afternoon, when I can best, having only one coachman, as ours are with Louis. At present they can't manage it often. . . .

October 3.

. . . Dr. Hofmeister is to both of us a source of real confidence and comfort. I don't think anyone else would have been more welcome to me just now, and he can write daily to Louis, and letters go usually in two days now.

I go as little as possible to the hospital now, and, indeed, do nothing imprudent, you can be sure. . . .

November 12.

. . . The nerves of my forehead and eyes are still painful; and from all sides I am again called upon to look after, settle, and advise concerning many things. On that account Dr. Weber and my mother-in-law insist on my leaving Darmstadt for a total change of scene, &c., for three weeks. I have resisted as long as I could, as I so much dislike going from home now (though I do not feel up to the work, and yet cannot keep from doing it), but I have finally given in, and accepted Vicky's kind invitation to accompany her for three weeks to Berlin. The journey is long and cold, but her company when we are both alone is a pleasure to me, and I shall hear all news as directly there as here.

. . . Last night I was much overcome. I had been sitting at the bedside of one of my poor young friends, and he was gasping in a too-distressing way. The father held his hand, the tears streaming down his cheek, the son trying to say "Weine nicht, Papa"

["Don't weep, Papa!]. The poor old father, so proud
of his good and handsome child, is heartbroken,
and they are touchingly united and full of feeling
for each other. I would give anything to save his
life; but all efforts will, I fear, be in vain. Though
I have seen so many lately die hard deaths, and
heard and seen the grief of many heartbroken
widows and mothers, it makes my heart bleed anew
in each fresh case, and curse the wickedness of war
again and again.

Poor Baby can't be christened yet, as my parents-
in-law think Louis would not like it during his absence, so I shall wait. . . .

November 17.

. . . How I rejoice to hear that Leopold gains so
much strength, and that he can be about again as
usual. Will you kindly tell him in Louis' name and
mine (as I am still restricted in all writing and
reading), that we beg him to stand godfather to our
little son?* Baby is so nice and fat now, and thrives
very well. I think you would admire him, his features are so pretty, and he is so pink, and looks so

---

* Prince Frederick William, the "Frittie" of these letters,
born the 6th of the previous month of October, and who was
killed by a fall from a window on the 29th of May, 1873.

wide-awake and intelligent. Ernie, who in general is a rough boy, is most tender and gentle to his little brother, and not jealous. . . .

Berlin: December 5.

. . . Yesterday Fieldmarshal Wrangel came to see me, and his words were, "Zu gratuliren, dass Ihr Mann ein Held ist, und sich so superb geschlagen hat" ["Accept my congratulations that your husband is a hero, and has fought so magnificently"]. I am very proud of all this, but I am too much a woman not to long above all things to have him safe home again.

. . . The evenings Vicky and I spend alone together, talking or writing our letters. There is so much to speak of and think about, of the present and the future, that it is to me a great comfort to be with dear Vicky. It is nearly five months since Louis left, and we lead such single existences that a sister is inexpressibly dear when all closer intercourse is so wanting! There is so much, beloved Mama, I should like to speak to you about. . . .

The girls are quite well, and very happy with their grandparents. The governess—who in the end did not suit for the children—as the six months' trial is over, will not remain, and I am looking for another one.

Darmstadt: December 18.

. . . The children and I bore the journey well, and it was not cold. Parting from dear Vicky was a hard moment, and I shall feel the loneliness here so much, and miss my dear good Louis more than ever. The children are, of course, at such a time the greatest blessing. There is so much to do for them and to look after for them; and mine are dear good children, and do not give over-much trouble.

Letters I have again received speak of the amount of danger Louis has again been daily exposed to, and how his personal courage and daring have given the victory in many a fight. God protect him! I live in fear and trembling for his precious life, and after I hear of his being safe through one battle, I take it as a fresh present from the Almighty, and breathe freer again, though the fear soon enough gets the upper hand again.

I have asked Uncle Louis to allow his *Berichte* [reports] to be copied for you. Louis has Köhler and another footman with him, that is all—and two coachmen. He rides at all battles the horse you gave him in 1866, which he rode during that campaign, and which is quite invaluable. It would interest Colonel Maude* to know this, as he bought

* Crown Equerry to the Queen.

the horse. My nursery is in very good order, and
they are all invaluable in their way.

How is good Dr. Hofmeister's family. Please
say many kind things to him from me, and tell him
that the Baby is getting so nice and fat, and is so
healthy in spite of all troubles. Here is a photograph of him, but not at all flattered. Please give
Dr. Hofmeister one of them!

I have this instant received a letter from Louis
dated the 11th! I will have an extract made for
you. I think it might interest Bertie to hear something of Louis, whom he can be proud to have as
a brother-in-law, for I hear his praises continually.
He has been throughout the war, as every other
General has been, without a carriage, &c., like other
Princes, and has gained the respect and devotion of
his troops.

Darmstadt: December 19.

. . . I hope for this last time, if we are spared
and live to come over together once more, we may
have the joy of showing their dear Grandmama
the whole little band. Of course, no thoughts of
plans can be entertained, and I know, after so very
long a separation, Louis would not be willing again
to part from his children.

My wounded were so pleased to see me again
yesterday.   Alas! many in bed, and so ill still! My
two in the house are much better, and the one who
during six weeks lay at death's door is recovering.
I have seldom experienced so great a satisfaction
as seeing this young man recover, and the doctors
say I have been the means of saving his life.

The joy of the old parents will be very great.
Since I left, there are new widows and fresh parents
bereft of only children; it is a most painful duty to
go to them.   But I know the comfort of sympathy
is the only one in deep grief.

December 23.

My warmest and tenderest thanks for your dear
and loving letter, with so many expressions of a
mother's love and sympathy, which do my heart
good, now that I feel so lonely and anxious.   It
seems too great a happiness to think of, that of our
being allowed to come with our children to you,
and to Scotland; and you know the smallest corner
is enough for us, who are by no means particular
—neither are our people. If I write this to Louis,
it will be something for him to look forward to, to
cheer him and reward him after so hard a time,
which he bears so bravely and uncomplainingly.
This morning I have been at the Alice Hospital,

which is prospering. I have been taking my gifts
for Christmas to one hospital after another. Your
two capes have delighted the poor sufferers, and
the one wounded for the second time is very bad,
alas! My wounded officer in the house is recovering, next to a miracle. For the two wounded in
the house, the children, our household, and the children of our servants at the war, I arrange Christmas
trees.

We grown-up ones of the family have given up
keeping Christmas for ourselves. We have too much
to do for others, and my parents-in-law, like me,
feel the absence of the dear ones who are always
here for Christmas.

I am superintending Victoria and Ella's letters
to you, which have not achieved the perfection
wished for. As they are to be quite their own,
I hope you will excuse their arriving a little
later.

Darmstadt: December 27.

. . . Louis telegraphed on Christmas day from
Orleans, where I had sent Christa's brother with a
box of eatables and woollen things for his people,
and a tiny Christmas tree with little lights for the
whole party. Louis has sent me a photograph of
himself and staff done at Orleans, and I have sent

for a copy for you, as it is very good. On Christmas day it was five months since Louis and the
troops left. The charming stockings you sent, I
have sent off in part to-day to Louis to give to his
Stabswache [Staff-guard]; the other things I divide
among the wounded and sick.

My children are all well. The little one sits up,
and, though not very fat, is round and firm, with
rosy cheeks and the brightest eyes possible. He is
very healthy and strong, and in fact the prettiest of
all my babies. The three girls are so grown, particularly the two eldest, you would scarcely know
them. They are both very tall for their age. Victoria is the height of Vicky's Charlotte, and Ella
not much less. They are thin, and a change of air
would be very beneficial.

1871.

Darmstadt: January 7.

. . . In England people are, I fear, becoming unjust towards the German troops. Such a long and bloody war must demoralise the best army; and I only say, in such a position how would the French have behaved? Many French officers say the same, and how greatly they respect the German soldier. Hundreds of French officers and two generals have broken their word of honour, and run away. I doubt whether *one* in the German army would do such a thing. The French peasants, often women, murder our soldiers in their beds, and the wounded they have used too horribly many a time. Is it a wonder, then, when the men let a feeling of revenge lay hold of them? A guerrilla war is always horrid, and no words can say how all Germans feel and deplore the present phase of the war! I hope and trust that the end may not be far distant.

One of the poor wounded soldiers whom I gave your cape to is dying, and the poor boy won't part from it for an instant, and holds it tight round himself.

Louis continues at Orleans, where they have entrenched themselves, and await with impatience news from Paris which must be of great influence for the continuation or ending of the war.

My days fly past. The children take much of my time—so, too, the house, my two wounded in the house, and the hospitals, to one of which I go daily.

Darmstadt: January 14.

. . . How kind of you to work something for Louis; he will wear it with such pleasure. Prince Frederick Carl's recent victories * and the fresh hosts of prisoners must help to bring the war to an end. Germany does not wish to go on, but the French won't see that they are beaten, and they will have to accept the visitors, who must increase in numbers the longer the French refuse to accede to the German demands.

I am so low, so deeply grieved for the misery entailed on both sides, and feel for the French so much. Our troops do not pillage in the way de-

---

* On the 10th, 11th, and 12th of January, 1871, before Le Mans.

scribed in English papers. I have read far worse accounts of what the French soldiers and *franc-tireurs* do in their French villages.

The poor soldier who had your cape is dead. He died with it round him. I was with him in the afternoon, and he had tears in his eyes, and was very low. In the night he died. This morning I was at the station to give things to the wounded and sick who came through—a sorry sight. This afternoon I am going to a poor soldier's widow who has just had twins. The distress on all sides is great. I help where I can. Becker tears his hair. The two wounded in the house cost so much. So does everything else; but as long as I can, through sparing on myself, help others, I must do it—though I have, as things are now, nothing left.

I will get a head of Ernest done for your brace-let, and another one, so that you may have something else of him. He is a magnificent boy, but so huge—such limbs! The Baby is not at all small, but near Ernest all the others look small.

He can't speak properly yet, but he understands everything, and has a wonderful ear for music. He sings the "Guten Kameraden" without a fault in the time, and is passionately fond of dancing, which he also does in time.

Irène is growing fast also, but the two eldest

7 *

are quite big girls; it makes me feel old when I see
them growing up to me so fast. Victoria has a very
inquiring mind, and is studious, and learns easily
and well. Since the middle of December I have
been without a governess.

To-morrow I go to Mayence to see poor Woldemar* Holstein's sister. He is very bad, to the grief
of all Mayence, and of all who know him.

Darmstadt: January 16.

My little Baby ought to be christened, but Louis
and my parents-in-law always hope that the end of
hostilities is near, and that Louis can then get leave.
Baby's blue eyes are beginning to turn, and look
almost as if they would be brown. Should dear
Grandmama's and Grandpapa's eyes come up again
amongst some of the grandchildren, how nice it
would be!

I have but little news to give. I go about to the
poor soldiers' widows and wives—no end of them,
with new-born babies, in the greatest distress.

Yesterday I saw the mother of the poor young
soldier who died. She keeps your cape as a

---

* Prince Henry Charles Woldemar of Schleswig-Holstein,
Governor of the fortress of Mayence. He died on the 20th of
January, 1871.

precious relic, as it had given him such great pleasure.

January 30.

Your charming photograph and kind letter arrived this morning—thousand thanks for both! How like the photograph, and how pleasing! I am so glad to have it.

The armistice and capitulation of Paris are great events. The people are out of their minds with joy —flags all over the town, and the streets crowded.

I forgot to say in my last letter how grieved I was about Beaty Durham's * death. It is quite shocking! and those numbers of children in so short a time. I earnestly hope none of us run such a chance, for on the whole our children have not been so close together. My last came sooner than I wished, and is smaller than his brother, but I hope now for a long rest. I have Baby fed, besides, so as not to try my strength. He is very healthy and strong, and is more like Victoria and my brothers and sisters than my other children, and his eyes remind me of Uncle Ernest's, and seem turning brown, which would be very pretty, as he is very fair otherwise.

* Daughter of the Duke of Abercorn.

Your pretty photograph is standing before me, and makes me quite absent. I catch myself continually staring at it, instead of writing my letters.

Darmstadt: February 2.

. . . All the many French here are pleased at the capitulation of Paris, and hope that peace is certain. Louis writes to me that the inhabitants of Orleans were equally pleased, and consider the war over. I earnestly pray it may be so. How greatly relieved and thankful all Germany would be!

Louis telegraphed to-day. He has no leave as yet, though he hopes for it. Now that there is a prospect of peace, and that the fighting is momentarily over, I feel quite a collapse of my nerves, after the strain that has been on them for six whole months. I can scarcely imagine what it will be when my beloved Louis is at home again; it seems *too great* a joy! Rest and quiet together are what I long for; and I fear in the first weeks he will have so much to do, and there will be much going on.

He speaks with the greatest hope of going to Scotland this autumn; and, if we are spared to do so, it will be such a rest, and do good to our healths, which must feel the wear and tear sooner or later.

February 11.

Many thanks for your last kind letter. I thought so much of you yesterday, spending the dear 10th for the first time again at Windsor. To-day our little son is to be christened, but only the family will be present, and my ladies and the two wounded gentlemen, who can get about on crutches now. When I think that the one owes his life to being here, it always gives me pleasure.

Two nights ago I was awakened by a dreadful noise, the whole house and my bed rocking from it; and twice again, though less violently. It was an earthquake, and I think too unpleasant. It frightens one so; the doors and windows rattle and shake. To-night two slight shocks, and one during the day yesterday.

How I shall miss dear Louis to-day! The seven months will be round ere we meet, I fear, and he has never seen his dear little boy. It always makes me sad to look at him, though now I have every reason to hope—please God—that I shall have the joy of seeing Louis come home, and of placing his baby in his arms. My heart is full, as you can fancy, and, much as I long to see Louis, I almost dread the moment—the emotion will be so great, and the long pent-up feelings will find vent.

I pray that peace may be restored, and that I

may not live to see *such* a war again, or to see my sons have to go to it.

I will tell Christa to write an account to you of the christening, for Leopold to see also, as he will be godfather. Frederic William Augustus (after the Empress) Victor (victory) Louis will be his names. Fritz and Vicky, the Empress and Fritz Carl, are godparents.

Darmstadt: February 14.

My bad eyes must again excuse the shortness of these lines, which are to thank you many times for your last dear letter.

Christa will have sent you the account of little Fritz's christening, which was a sad day for me, and will have been so for dear Louis likewise. We have added dear Leopold's name to the others, as his sad life, and the anxiety his health has so often caused us all, endear him particularly, and we hoped it would give him pleasure, dear boy.

The elections in the provinces are all for peace, and only the towns for war and a republic. This week is one of intense and anxious expectation; though the greater portion believe in the restoration of peace, yet we have no security for it.

March 6.

. . . Now dear Louise's marriage draws near,
how much you must feel it! I think so much of
her, of your and of my dear home. I trust she will
be very happy, which with such an amiable young
man she must be.

Louis has received the Order "Pour le mérite,"
which I am so glad of for him. The Emperor telegraphed the announcement to my mother-in-law,
with many complimentary words about her sons.
To have the three sons safe is something to be
thankful for, for they were much and continually
exposed. I know nothing of Louis' coming. The
troops march home, and it will take at least six
weeks. I hope so much that he may have leave for
a fortnight, and then return to the troops, to lead
them home.

To-night are the peace illuminations here, which
will be very pretty. Our house will also be illumin-
ated, and I take the two eldest girls out with me
to-night to see it all. It is a thing for them never
to forget, this great and glorious, though too horrid,
war.

March 13.

I know nothing as yet of Louis' return. I fear
I must wait a few weeks longer. On Wednesday

the Emperor, Fritz, and some of the Princes pass through Frankfort, and I am going there with my parents-in-law to see them.

The Paris news is not very edifying, and I fear France has not seen the worst yet, for there seems to be a fearful state of anarchy there.

I have no news to give, save that Frittie has his first tooth. He is between Victoria and Irène, but not like Ernie—not near so big, which is really not necessary. I think he is the sort of baby you admire. I go on looking after my hospitals, and now the trains, full of Landwehr returning home cheering and singing, begin to pass. Now good-bye, darling Mama. I am in thought daily with you during these days, and only wish it had been in my power to be of any use or comfort to you just now.

Darmstadt: April 8.

. . . We had the pleasure of catching a glimpse of Louise and Lorne on their way through, but their stay was too short to be able to say more than a few words. They can scarcely help passing through here, as they can't go through France, on their way back; and if you would allow them *quite incognito* on their way back to pass a day here, it would give both Louise and me the greatest pleasure, and entail no other visits.

The Emperor, who kindly gave Louis leave, prolonged it till Monday, when he leaves, and for how long is quite undecided. If I could only go with him! Marie of Saxony has joined George: so has Carola [the Crown Princess of Saxony] her husband; but our division, which is near Chaumont, is in too bad and close quarters to admit of my living there.

Should Louis have to remain very long, I still hope to rejoin him—I don't care about the little discomfort.

The new governess, Frl. Kitz, comes on Thursday. She is not young, but pleasing-looking—said to be very amiable, and a good governess; has been for eighteen years in England, first with Lady Palk, and then for ten years with Herr Kleinwart—a rich German banker in London—where she brought up the two daughters.

Darmstadt: April 13.

. . . Ernie's kilt was sent him by Mr. Mitchell. * He admired Ernie so much at Berlin, that he said he would send him a Scotch dress, and I could not

* The late Mr. John Mitchell, the librarian of Old Bond Street.

refuse. It is rather small as it is, and I hope that you will still give him one, as from his Grandmama it would be doubly valuable.

Louis has arrived safely at his destination—Donjeux; and we both feel the separation very much after having had the happiness of being together again.

The Paris battles are too dreadful, and the end seems some way off yet.

May 27.

My thoughts cannot leave unfortunate Paris! What horrors, and enacted so close by in the centre of the civilised world! It seems incredible; and what a lesson for those who wish to learn by it!

Darmstadt: June 8.

Louise and Lorne are just gone, and it rains and blows, and is dreadful. Their visit was so pleasant, so *gemüthlich*, and I think Louise looks well and happy. She had much to tell of their journey, which seems to have been very interesting. I could show them almost nothing, as the weather was so bad. We three went yesterday evening to my parents-in-law, who were most kind to them, as they always are to all my relations.

Their short stay was a great *great* pleasure to

me, so cut off from home as I have been since three long years.

Louis will be here in a few days, and we go together to Berlin for four days; Louis insists on my accompanying him. On the 24th the entry of the troops will be here.

Seeheim: June 14.

. . . I am so glad that the poor Emperor and Empress are so kindly treated. They deserve to be well used by England, for the Emperor did so much to bring France and England together. How shamefully the French treat them, and speak of them, is not to be told; for the French consider themselves blameless, and always betrayed by others, whom they had made almost their gods of as long as all went well.

Dear Frittie is getting better—principally his looks, but the illness is not overcome yet. I have been so anxious about him. The country here is more beautiful than ever, and country air and flowers are a great enjoyment. Every little walk is up and down hill, little brooks, rocks, small green valleys, fine woods, &c. I have not lived here since 1865, when Ella was a baby. The children are beside themselves with pleasure at the pretty country and the scrambling walks, but above all at the wild flowers, in which they are getting quite learned. I find them in a book for them, and even Ernie knows some names, and never calls them wrong. All my children are great lovers of nature, and I develop this as much as I can. It makes life so rich, and they can never feel dull anywhere, if they know to seek and find around them the thousand beauties and wonders of nature. They are very happy and contented, and always see, the less people have the less they want, and the greater is the enjoyment of that which they have. I bring my children up as simply and with as few wants as I can, and, above all, teach them to help themselves and others, so as to become independent.

Darmstadt: June 20.

Thousand thanks for your dear letter received before our departure from Potsdam! Our journey was dreadful. We left in the evening, and were to have been here at 11 A.M., and through the irregularity of the trains we only got here at four in the afternoon. I am quite done up. The fatigues at Berlin were incessant. Anything more grand, more imposing or touching and *erhebend* [elevating] than the entry of the troops in Berlin I never saw. It was a wonderful sight to drive for three-quarters of an hour through rows of French cannon! The decorations were so artistic, so handsome, and the enthusiasm of the dense crowds quite enormous. I am glad to have been there: it will be a thing to recollect. The old Emperor, surrounded by the many princes and by his great generals, looked so noble riding at the head of his glorious troops. Deputations of all the German troops were there.

It was very hot, and we had to drive every day to Berlin, and back in the evening.

Alas! it is rainy here, and the town is so beautifully decorated: three large triumphal arches, and the houses covered with garlands and flags.

I found the dear children well, though rather pale from the heat.

Louis left again this morning, but after to-morrow remains here for good, which will indeed be a pleasure after such endless separations.

Darmstadt: June 27.

. . . To-day Aunt Marie * of Russia and her children were here. Aunt Marie looks thinner than ever, but well; and Marie dear and nice, with such a kind fresh face, so simple and girlish. She gives her brothers music lessons during the journey,

---

* Empress of Russia, mother of the Duchess of Edinburgh, and aunt of Prince Louis of Hesse.

which she is very proud of. She is very fond of
children, and of a quiet country life—that is the
ideal she looks for. The Emperor of Russia comes
here on the 5th, to join Aunt Marie at Petersthal.
Louis' work is incessant—the selling off of horses,
the changing garrisons of the regiments, the new
formation of our division, causes almost more work
than the *Mobilmachung* [mobilisation]. The entry
was very beautiful: the decorations of the town
most tasteful; not a house or the smallest street
which was not covered with garlands, flags, and em-
blems. There were large groups of the captured
guns, and the names of the battles on shields
around. Unfortunately, it poured nearly all the
time, and we were quite drenched. I had the five
children in my carriage, and Irène gave wreaths to
her godfathers of the cavalry brigade. Two days
ago we gave a large military dinner, and have
several soirées of that sort to give before we can go
into the country, which I am longing for. We shall
probably go to Seeheim, as the summer seems too
damp for Kranichstein.

The middle of August we shall go to Blankenberghe, near Ostend, as the doctors wish sea-bathing
for Louis, and sea air for me and for some of the
children, which is very necessary to set us up before going to Scotland. We want to remain one or

two days and one night in London. We require a few things, which make a stay necessary. If we might be at Balmoral on the 10th, as Louis's birthday is on the 12th, would that suit you?

Please let me know in time if you think our plans good. This will enable us to settle when to go to Blankenberghe, as we can't be there longer than three weeks.

How I look forward to seeing you again, and to come home once more! It is so kind of you to let us bring the children. The arrangement of the rooms will do perfectly, and we don't care how we are put up, and above all things don't wish to be in the way.

The weather is horrid—rain and wind incessantly—after having been tremendously hot. These sudden changes upset everyone, and Frittie has had a very slight return of his illness.

August 13.

We leave at eight to-morrow morning, reach Cologne at one o'clock, and wait there till ten in the evening, when we continue our journey and reach Blankenberghe at eight next morning. Will you kindly send a gentleman to Gravesend, who can remain with us in London, as we are quite alone?

Uncle George, Aunt Cambridge, and Mary dined with us at Frankfort two days ago. Mary I had not seen for three years; she was looking very handsome.

Blankenberghe: August 17.

Only two words to say that we arrived safe and well here yesterday after a very hot journey. The hotel is on the beach, where we sit all day; there are no walks or anything save the beach, and no trees. Our rooms are very small and not very clean; but the heavenly sea air and the wind refresh one, and the sands are very long. One can ride on donkeys which enchants young and old children. Everyone bathes together, and one has to take a little run before the waves cover one. We bathed with the three girls this morning, but I felt quite shy, for all the people sit round and look on, and there are great numbers of people here. Our children play about with others and dig in the sand. Frittie sleeps so well since he has been here; his colour is beginning to return.

We have one small sitting-room, which is our dining-room, and Louis's dressing-room.

I was so sad and upset at taking leave of my

dear Marie* Grancy the other day; a kind true friend and companion has she been to me these nine years, and during the war she was quite invaluable to me. I hope she will be as happy as she deserves to be.

Buckingham Palace: September 10.

The pleasure of seeing your dear handwriting again has been so great! Thank God that you are going on well. I do feel *so much* for you, and for all you have had to suffer in every way! I trust entire quiet and rest of mind and body, and any little attention that I may be able to offer for your comfort, will make the autumn of real benefit for your health. How I do look forward to seeing you again, I can't say. . . .

We propose leaving the evening of the 13th. Bertie and Uncle George have arranged for our going to Aldershot on Monday and Tuesday, which interests Louis above all things, and I fancied this arrangement would suit you best.

The journey has quite cured Frittie, without any medicine, and the heat is over.

. . . I took Victoria and Ella to the Exhibition,

* Lady in Waiting to the Princess, married to General v. Hesse.

and what enchanted Ella most was a policeman,
who was, as she said, "so very kind" in keeping the
crowd off. It reminded me of "Susy Pusy," which
dear Papa used to tease me with as a child.

We dined and lunched with Bertie, who had
only just arrived, and is gone again. Dear Arthur
of course I have not seen.

Bram's Hill Park Camp, Cavalry Brigade, 2nd Division:
September 12.

In Bertie's tent I write these few lines to thank
you in Louis's name and my own a thousand times
for your dear kind letter. Every loving word is so
precious to us, and the presents you so kindly gave
Louis enchanted him. The pin, unfortunately, did
not arrive.

How I regret each time I hear you speak of your
illness! I have been so anxious about you. Uncle
Louis and my parents-in-law, in their telegram of
to-day, inquire after you.

We have had two such interesting days; the
country too lovely, each day in a quite different
part. We accompanied Uncle George, and in this
way have seen the two Divisions, and through sleeping here will be enabled to see the third Division
to-morrow before returning to town.

I saw dear Arthur yesterday. He rode with me all the time, and to-day we met him marching with his company. How I have enjoyed seeing your splendid troops again, I can't tell you; but I shall reserve all news till we meet.

Louis thanks you again and again for your kindness, and only regrets not having seen you himself, but is very grateful that we were allowed to stay a few days at Buckingham Palace, through which we were enabled to come here, which to him as a soldier is of the very greatest interest. Bertie is full of his work, and I think it interests him immensely. He has charming officers about him, to help and show him what to do. To our great disappointment we did not see the 42nd Highlanders, the "Black Watch," to-day; but yesterday we saw the Argyle-shire 91st Highlanders, who gave Louise the present. Bertie lent me a charming little horse, but the ground is dreadful, and not having ridden for so long, and being on horseback so many hours, makes me feel quite stiff.

Dunrobin Castle, Sutherland: October 19.

I wish your telegram had brought me better news of you. I really can't bear to think of you suffering, and so much alone. I feel it quite wrong to have left you, and my thoughts and wishes are continually with you, and distract my attention from all I see here. I can't tell you how much I feel for you at being so helpless. It is such a trial to anyone so active as yourself; but your trial must be drawing to a close, and you will be rewarded in the end, I am sure, by feeling perhaps even better and stronger than you did before all your troubles.

I was nearly sick in the train, which is the slowest I was ever in in my life, and was unable to go to dinner; but a long walk by the sea this morning has quite set me up in spite of the extraordinary warmth.

Sandringham: November 9.

It is the first time since eleven years that I have spent Bertie's birthday with him, and though we are only three of our own family together, still that is better than nothing, and makes it seem more like birthday. Bertie and Alix are so kind, and give us so warm a welcome, showing how they like having us, that it feels quite home. Indeed I pray earnestly that God's blessing may rest on him, and that he may be guided to do what is wise and right, so that he may tide safely through the anxious times that are before him, and in which we now live. They are both charming hosts, and all the party suit well together. The Westminsters and Brownlows are here; Lady B. is so very handsome.

We joined the shooting party for luncheon, and the last beats out to-day and yesterday; and the weather is beautiful, though cold—a very bracing air, like Scotland.

———

1872.

Darmstadt: January 21.

. . . Louis returns to-morrow from Berlin. He was the first to be invested by the Emperor, and has met with great kindness. He was very glad to have been there with dear Arthur, who seems to please everyone.

February 5.

. . . It is a great pleasure to have dear Arthur here. He is so amiable, civil, and nice, and takes interest in all he sees, and is so pleasant to have in the house. His visit will be very short, as he gives up two days to go to Baden.

We gave small suppers on two evenings for Arthur, and yesterday evening a celebrated most excellent violinist played quite as well as Joachim: a friend of his, and a pupil of Spohr's. This afternoon he is going to play some of Bach's celebrated sonatas with and to me. Arthur enjoys music very much, and keeps up his playing.

There is a dance at Uncle Alexander's to-night, on Wednesday a Court ball, and on Friday one at my parents-in-law. I can't stand the heat at all of an evening, and the rooms are very hot. Louis, who has an awful cold, took Arthur to see the barracks, as all military things give him pleasure.

It is heavenly sunny weather, having been quite dark and foggy all day yesterday.

June 17.

Many thanks for your dear letter and kind wishes for the birth of our Baby*—a nice little thing, like Ella, only smaller and with finer features, though the nose promises to be long. . . .

Kind Dr. Hofmeister was most attentive; and of course having him was far pleasanter than not, and we owe you great thanks for having sent him. Mrs. Clarke has been all one could wish.

Louis wrote as soon as he could, but this last week he has only been home just before his dinner, and was so tired that he invariably fell asleep. He has gone out at six, returning at twelve, and has had to be out before four in the afternoon, returning at eight. He is away again to-day. Until the 15th of September his duty will be important, and

* Princess Alix, born on the 6th of June.

he has all the office work besides. It is double this year to what it usually is, as all people and things are new since the war.

How sad the loss of those two poor children is,* and the sweet little "bairnie" of three! The unfortunate mother to lose two in so dreadful a way! I am sure it touched Beatrice much to see the poor little one; and in a child death so often loses everything that is painful.

We think of calling our little girl "Alix" (Alice they pronounce too dreadfully in German) "Helena Louise Beatrice," and, if Beatrice may, we would much like to have her as godmother.

Darmstadt: June 24.

. . . We both felt so truly for you when we heard of dear Dr. Macleod's death, knowing what a kind and valued friend of yours he was, and how fate seems to take one friend after another, and before age can claim its right. He indeed deserves his rest, for he did so much good in his life!

---

* Two children who were carried away by a "spate" while playing in Monaltrie Burn, near Balmoral (11th of June, 1872), and swept into the river Dee and drowned. See *More Leaves from a Journal of a Life in the Highlands*, pp. 128 *et seq.*

I feel rather weaker than usual this time, and sitting and walking, though only a few steps, tries me a good deal. I was out for half an hour yesterday, and I think the air will do me good.

Louis left at half-past five this morning, and will be back by seven, I hope, this evening; to-morrow the same.

I will add Vicky's name to Baby's others, as you propose; and "Alix" we gave for "Alice," as they murder my name here: "Aliicé" they pronounce it, so we thought "Alix" could not so easily be spoilt.

Uncle Alexander is coming back shortly, and says the Empress is not to return to Russia this winter, and will be sent to Italy for the whole winter.

The heat has been quite dreadful; there is a little air to-day, though.

August 14.

. . . Baby is like Ella, only smaller features, and still darker eyes with very black lashes, and reddish-brown hair. She is a sweet, merry little person, always laughing, with a deep dimple in one cheek just like Ernie.

We are going to Frankfort to-day to give Uncle

George* and Fritz Strelitz** a luncheon in our Palais there. Hélène Reuter comes to us for a month to-morrow as lady.

I hope your Edinburgh visit will go off well. You have never lived in Holyrood since 1861, have you?

How I shall think of you at dear Balmoral, and this time capable of enjoying it—not like last time, when you had to suffer so much, and were unable to do anything. It quite spoiled our visit to see you an invalid. Remember me to all old friends there—to Brown's kind old mother, and any who ask after us.

I shall think of you on dear Grandmama's birthday. She is never forgotten by any of us, and lives on as a dearly-cherished memory of all that was good and loving, and so kind. My children have her picture in their room, and I often tell them of her.

Kranichstein: August 20.

I am very grateful for your telegrams from Edinburgh, and for Flora* [MacDonald's] letter. It in-

---

* Duke of Cambridge.
** Grand Duke of Mecklenburg Strelitz.
*** Maid of Honour to the Queen, now Bedchamber Woman.

terests me so much to know what you did there, and I am very glad all went off so well. The people will have been too delighted to have had you in their midst again, and I am sure you enjoyed the beauty of your fine northern capital anew after not having seen it for so long a time. Beatrice seems delighted with what she saw. I recollect those many interesting and beautiful spots so well.*

The 18th was the anniversary of the dreadful battle of Gravelotte, which cost so many lives, to our division especially. We drove into town to the military church, which was full of officers and men, at half-past seven in the morning, and thought much of the friends and acquaintances in their distant graves, and of the desolate homes, until that day so bright. My heart felt too full when we were singing *Ein' feste Burg*, and I had my husband at my side, whom the Almighty had graciously spared to my children and myself. Gratitude seems barely enough to express the intense depth of what I feel when I think of that time, and how again and again I long to give all and all to my good dear Louis and to our children, for he is all that is good and true and pure.

---

* For an account of this visit, see *More Leaves from a Journal* pp. 133 *et seq.*

. . . The children were much distressed at the sad fate of my poor little bullfinch, who piped beautifully. Louis had caught an owl and put it in a wooden sort of cage in the room where my bird was. In the night it broke the bars and got loose and tore the bullfinch's tail out, and the poor little thing died in consequence.

Of our quiet country life there is little to tell. We are a good deal out always with our little people, their pets—dogs, cats, ponies, donkeys; it is rather like a menagerie.

Schloss Kranichstein: September 17.

On the 9th there is a large meeting here of the different associations existing throughout Germany for the bettering of women's education and social position (of the middle class especially with regard to trade). Some English ladies are coming, some Swiss and Dutch. It will last four days, and be very fatiguing. The programme I arranged with my two committees here and the gentlemen at Berlin, and they wanted to force me to preside; but for so large an assemblage—to me nearly all strangers—I positively refused. I do that in my own Associations, but not where there are so many strangers, who all want to talk, and all to cross purposes. It is difficult enough to keep one's own people in order when they disagree. I hope and trust I have prevented *all* exaggerated and unfeminine views being brought up, which to me are dreadful. These Associations, if not reasonably led, tend too easily to the ridiculous. My Associations take a great deal of my time and thought, and require a good amount of study. I hope and trust that what we are doing here is the right thing. We have already had some satisfactory results in the class of the workwomen, and in the reform of the schools; but there are many open questions yet, which I hope this meeting, with others who work in the same field, may help us to solve.

Will you look through the programme? It would please me so much if I thought you took a little interest in my endeavours here in a very small way to follow in a slight degree part of dear Papa's great works for the good of others.

Kranichstein: September 25.

. . . *All* sympathise with you, and feel what a loss to you darling Aunt* must be—how great the

---

* The Queen's half-sister, Feodore, Princess of Hohenlohe-Langenburg, who died on the 23rd of September, 1872, at Baden-Baden.

gap in your life, how painful the absence of that sympathy and love which united her life and yours so closely.

Darling, kind Mama, I feel so acutely for you, that my thoughts are incessantly with you, and my prayers for comfort and support to be granted you in the heavy trial are warm indeed. You have borne so many hard losses with courage and resignation, that for darling Aunt's sake you will do so again, and knowing her at rest and peace will in time reconcile you to the loss—all the more as her passing from this world to another was so touchingly peaceful. Dear Augusta [Stanley] wrote to me, which was a great consolation, and we intend going to Baden to pay our last token of respect and love.

Darmstadt: October 13.

. . . A few words about our doings here may be of interest to you. The meeting went off well, was very large, the subjects discussed to the purpose and important, and not one word of the emancipated political side of the question was touched upon by anyone. Schools (those of the lower, middle, and higher classes) for girls were the principal theme; the employment of women for post and telegraph offices, &c.; the improvement necessary in the education of nursery-maids, and the knowledge of mothers in the treatment of little children; the question of nurses and nursing institutes.

The committees of the fifteen Associations met Wednesday afternoon, and in the evening thirteen of the members came to us to supper.

The public meeting on the following day lasted from nine to two with a small interruption; a committee meeting in the afternoon; and that evening all the members and guests came to us—nearly fifty in number. The following day the meetings lasted even longer, and the English ladies were kind enough to speak—only think, old Miss Carpenter, on all relating to women's work in England (she is our guest here). Her account of the Queen's Institute at Dublin was most interesting. Miss Hill (also our guest), about the boarding-out system for orphans. Miss C. Winkworth, about higher education in England. She mentioned also the new institution to which Louise now belongs, and is a member of it herself. The ladies all spoke very well; the German ones remarkably so.

There was a good deal of work to finish afterwards, and a good many members to see. They came from all parts of Germany—many kind-hearted, noble, self-denying women. The presence of the English ladies—above all, of one such as

Miss Carpenter, who has done such good works for the reformation of convicts—greatly enhanced the importance of the meeting, and her great experience has been of value to us all. She means still to give a lecture on India and the state of the native schools there, before leaving us.

I have still so much work in hand, that I fear my letter is hurried and ill-written, but I hope you will kindly excuse this.

To-morrow I am taking Miss Carpenter to all our different schools, that she may see how the different systems in use work. Some are good, but none particularly so; there is much to improve.

Louis is gone to Mayence to-day for the inauguration of the Memorial which the town has erected to the memory of dear excellent Woldemar Holstein, for so many years its beloved Governor.

Darmstadt: October 24.

You must indeed miss dear Aunt much, and feel your thoughts drawn to her, whose precious intercourse was such a solace and comfort to you. It is nice for you to have Louise a little to yourself. . . .

You ask, if my mother-in-law talks with me about the different woman's work in which I am interested. Of course she does. We are so intimate together, that even where we differ in opinion we yet talk of everything freely, and her opinion is of the greatest value to me. She has ever been a most kind, true, and loving mother, whom I respect and love more and more. She was much pleased and interested in the success of the meeting, but is of course as averse as myself to all extreme views on such subjects.

I have joined to my Nursing Institute an Association for watching over the orphans who are boarded out by the State into families, where some poor children are unhappy and ill-used. The use of such meetings as this one was consists mainly in the interchange of experience made in the different branches in other places, which it is impossible to carry on by correspondence.

The schools are entirely different throughout Germany—good and indifferent; and those here do not count among the best, as everything, through the long misrule of the late Government, is not what it ought to be.

Darmstadt: November 3.

Ella is writing to you herself to thank you for the lovely bracelet, which gave me as much pleasure as it did her. To think that she is already eight!

9*

She is handsomer than she was, and a dear child.
. . . They all give me pleasure, dear children,
though of course they have as many faults as others;
but they are truthful and contented, and very affectionate. Having them much with me, watching
and guiding their education—which, through our
quiet and regular life, is possible—I am able to
know and understand their different characters, for
not one is like the other.

Darmstadt: November 12.

. . . We have the same weather here which you
seem to have, which for our long journey was not
pleasant. We took nearly twelve hours going, and
as much returning from Metz. For the inauguration
itself the weather held up. The roads were dreadful, and the wide plateau looked dreary and sad—
dotted all over with graves, like an enormous
churchyard.

The Memorial is a dead lion in bronze, on a
plain pedestal, bearing an inscription on black
marble in front, and at the back all the names.
Deputations of officers and men were present,
besides the generals, &c., from Metz. The clergy-
man of the division read the prayers, preached a
short and touching sermon, and the band played a
chorale. Louis spoke a few words, ending with the

usual "Hoch" for the Emperor and Grand Duke. I
then laid some wreaths at the foot of the Memorial
from Louis's parents and ourselves, and we drove
back to Metz across the different battlefields. The
villages are all built up again, and re-inhabited, so
that few traces of the dreadful struggle remain.

Darmstadt: December 12.

For the 14th I write a few words. From year
to year they can but express the same : the grief at
the loss of such a father, such a man, grows with
me, and leaves a gap and a want that nothing on
earth can ever fill up.

The deep, intense sympathy for what you, my
poor dear Mama, went through then and since, in
consequence of your bereavement, remains as vivid
as ever. God heard our prayers, and sustained
you, and through the healing hand of time softened
your grief, and retained you for us, who were too
young and too numerous to stand alone!

That our good sweet Alix should have been
spared this terrible grief, when this time last year
it seemed so imminent, fills my heart with gratitude
for her dear sake, as for yours, his children, and
ours. That time is as indelibly fixed on my memory
as that of 1861, when the witnessing of your grief

rent my heart so deeply. The 14th will now be a
day of mixed recollections and feelings to us—a
day *hallowed* in our family, when one great spirit
ended his work on earth—though his work can
never die, and generations will grow up and call
his name blessed—and when another was left to
fulfil his duty and mission, God grant, for the wel-
fare of his own family and of thousands!

I have not time to write to dearest Bertie and
Alix to-day; and as I love to think of them with
you on the 14th, so I would ask you to let them
share these lines full of sympathy for them, letting
a remembrance of *me*, who suffered with them,
mingle with your united prayers and thanks on this
solemn day!

My little Fritz is at length better, but white and
thin, in consequence of his illness.

Christmas Day.

Your dear presents gave me so much pleasure;
I thank you again and again for them. The precious
souvenir of dear Aunt, and my Ernie's picture
delight me. I assure you, nothing has given me
more pleasure this Christmas.

Let me also thank you, in Louis' and the children's names (meanwhile, until they do so themselves), for your kind gift to them. It makes us

all so happy and grateful, to be always so kindly remembered.

The boys were well enough to enjoy Christmas, though rather pale and pulled—above all, sweet Ernie.

We gave all our servants presents—the whole household and stable—under the Christmas-tree, which we made for the children; and when the tree is divided, the children of all our servants come and share it with ours. It keeps the household as a family, which is so important. We have fifty people to give to!

Dear Beatrice's wishes (cards) pleased the children very much, but Frittie lamented for a letter from Auntie "for Frittie." He talks quite well now.

On Saturday we shall go for the day to Vicky. I don't like leaving the boys for longer yet. I am so glad Vicky gave such a flattering account of Baby. She is quite the personification of her nickname "Sunny"—much like Ella, but a smaller head, and livelier, with Ernie's dimple and expression.

1873.

. . . We were both much shocked to hear of the
death of the Emperor Napoleon, and I must say
grieved; personally he was so amiable, and she is
much to be pitied. That he should die an exile
in England, as Louis Philippe did, is most striking.
In England the sympathy shown must touch the
poor Empress, and, as I telegraphed, we should be
so grateful to you, if you would kindly be the
medium through which both of us would like to
express to her how much we feel for her. How
proud you must ever be, in feeling that your country
is the one always able to offer a home and hos-
pitality for those driven away from their own
countries! England is before all others in that;
and its warm sympathy for those who are in misfortune is such a generous feeling.

February 1.

If anyone will feel with us, I know you will do
so most. Since three days, with an interruption of

one day, poor Frittie has been bleeding incessantly
from a slight cut on his ear, which was nearly
healed. Since yesterday evening we cannot stop
it. All the usual remedies were used, but as yet
unavailing. Just now the place has been touched
again with caustic, and tightly bound, after we had
with great trouble got rid of the quantity of dried
blood from his hair, ear, neck, &c. He is horrified
at the sight of so much blood, but shows great
strength as yet in spite of so great a loss. He is
of course very irritable, and, as he must not scream,
one has to do whatever he wishes, which will spoil
him dreadfully. I own I was much upset when I
saw that he had this tendency to bleed, and the
anxiety for the future, even if he gets well over
this, will remain for years to come. All have their
trials, one or another, and, please God, we shall
bear whatever is sent without complaining. To see
one's own child suffer is for a mother a great trial.
With what pleasure one would change places with
the little one, and bear its pain!

February 6.

. . . In the summer Fritz had a violent attack of
dysentery, which was so prevalent at Darmstadt,
and off and on for two months it continued, until

Scotland stopped it; and this illness made him
sensitive and delicate.

. . . What has caused him such great suffering
has been that, what with the use of caustic, the
tight bandaging and the iron, a quantity of small
gatherings formed on his cheek and neck, causing
such an amount of pain that he could not remain
in bed or anywhere quiet for the two first days and
nights. Now they are drying off, the itching is
such that he don't know what to do with himself,
and we have the greatest difficulty in keeping him
from rubbing or scratching himself. The want of
sleep through pain, &c., has excited him very much,
so that he has been very difficult to manage. The
bandages of course cannot be removed, and great
care will be taken when they are removed, lest
bleeding should recommence. He has been out
twice a day as usual all along, and his skin never
quite lost its pinkness and mottled appearance; all
of which are signs that he has good blood and to
spare, else he would look worse and have shown
weakness, which after all he did not. . . .

He speaks well for his age, and is, alas! very
wild, so that it will be impossible to keep him from
having accidents. . . .

. . . I have been playing some lovely things

(very difficult) of Chopin lately, which I know you would admire.

Darmstadt: February 19.

My best thanks for your dear letter! That I forgot to thank you at once for dear Grandmama's very beautiful print* came from my having the lithograph of that picture in my room always before me, and, though the print far surpasses it, I am so fond of the lithograph, that I forgot the print at the moment I was writing to you. Before that dear picture, the painting of which I recollect so well, my children often sit, and I tell them of her who was and ever will be so inexpressibly dear to us all. In the schoolroom, in my sitting-room, in the nursery, there is with the pictures of you and dear Papa always one of dear Grandmama, and, in my room and the schoolroom, the Duke of Kent also.

My sitting-room has only prints and lithographs, all Winterhalters, of the family: you and Papa, your receiving the Sacrament at the Coronation, Raphael's *Disputa* and *Belle Jardinière*, and the lovely little engraving of yourself from Winterhalter's picture in Papa's room at Windsor.**

* A private plate, engraved for the Queen by the late Mr. Francis Holl from a picture by Winterhalter.

** Also engraved by the late Mr. Francis Holl for the

Vicky is coming here on Wednesday. The Grand Duke of Weimar has kindly allowed Mr. Ruland* to join us as cicerone: which for galleries, &c., is very necessary, and we take no courier. Rome is our first halting-place in Italy, and for years it has been my dream and wish to be in that wonderful city, where the glorious monuments of antiquity and of the Middle Ages carry one back to those marvellous times.

I am learning Italian, and studying the history and art necessary to enable me, in the short time we have, to see and understand the finest and most important monuments. I am so entirely absorbed and interested in these studies just now, that I have not much time for other things. My father-in-law, perhaps Princess Charles too, will be with Aunt Marie of Russia at Sorrento then. William will probably join us at Rome; he is quite a connoisseur in art, and a good historian, quite at home in Rome, about which he raves. I must say that I look forward immensely to this journey; it opens a whole new life to one. . . .

Queen from a picture given by Her Majesty to the Prince Consort on the 26th of August, 1843.

   * Former German private secretary and librarian to the Prince Consort.

Kanné has made all arrangements for us at Rome. We shall leave here about the 18th of March.

Rome, Hôtel d'Allemagne: March 27.

. . . We left the dear children well, but very sorry at parting. The two days at Munich were most interesting. The National Museum in its way surpasses any I have ever seen, and in originals is richer even than South Kensington. Aunt Mariechen was very kind and dear; the Moriers very amiable hosts, and we met some interesting people there. Two hours before we left, after eight in the evening, Ludwig and Otto* came to us and remained some time.

The Brenner, over which we came, was covered with snow—most beautiful scenery, like St. Moritz in the Engadine. The journey was very fatiguing. We had a morning for Bologna, and had to wait three hours at Florence for the night train—time enough to drive round and in the town, which is most lovely. What trees, mountains, colours! then the fine buildings!

The following morning at six we reached Rome.

* The King of Bavaria and his brother, first cousins of Prince Louis of Hesse.

The sun was bright, the distance blue—the grand ruins dark and sharp against the sky, cypresses, stone-pines, large cork oaks, making up such a beautiful picture. Every day I admire the scenery more and more; every little bit of architecture, broken or whole, with a glimpse of the Campagna, a picturesque dirty peasant and a dark tree close by, is a picture in itself which one would like to frame and hang up in one's room. It is too, too beautiful! To tell you all we have seen and are seeing would tire you. Bertie and Arthur's descriptions, too, so lately have told you the same.

The Via Appia, the grand old road lined with ruins of splendid tombs, leading from Albano through the Campagna to Rome, along which St. Paul went, and the great kings and emperors made their triumphal entries, is a fit one to lead to such a city as Rome, which ruled the world.

The antique monuments, those of the Middle Ages, are so magnificent and interesting that as yet I don't know which to mention first or admire most!

Our incognito did not last long (though even now we maintain it), for the Crown Princess* heard

* Crown Princess of Italy, daughter of the Duke of Genoa, and granddaughter of late King of Saxony.

of us and came to see us, as did the Crown Prince, and we had to go to the Quirinal, a morning visit without *entourage*.

Palm Sunday, Rome: April 6.

. . . We saw the beginning of Mass and blessing of the palms in St. Peter's this morning, with a procession and beautiful singing. Whilst the procession, with part of the choristers, go outside the church, some remain within, and they respond to each other, which produces a very striking effect. In spite of the bad style inside of St. Peter's, as a whole it produces a marvellous effect through its wonderful size and richness of decoration.

I saw two convents yesterday: the Sepolte Vive, which Bertie and Alix saw, and where the nuns asked much after him, and said that he was *molto amabile;* and another equally strict one, but not austere, where the Superior told me that Aunt Feodore with Princess Hohenzollern had paid them a visit. Monsignore Howard was the only gentleman with me and the ladies, as they never see any men. Their idea is, that they spend the whole of their life in contemplation and prayer, so as to pray for those who cannot pray for themselves.

The museums of the Vatican and of the Capitol, with their enormous collection of antiques, are very fine. The celebrated Venus, Apollo Belvedere, the Torso (which Michael Angelo admired so much, and was taken to touch when he could no more see it), the wounded Gladiator, &c., are there. The Sistine Chapel, with Michael Angelo's frescoes, which are certainly the most marvellous pieces of painting and conception, is very dark, and the frescoes are suffering much from the smoke, dust, &c. Raphael's Stanze are far better preserved, and lighter than I had expected, and of such beauty!

I thought so often and so much of dear Papa when I saw the originals of all the pictures he so much admired and took such interest in. How this alone fascinates me I cannot tell you. In these galleries and churches there is only too much to be seen, besides the antique ruins, &c. You would be terrified to see how full our day is from before nine. Mr. Ruland is an excellent cicerone for pictures and sculptures. William is with us here since last Sunday.

We are going to the Villa Ludovisi this afternoon. The gardens of the Villa Doria Pamfili are most beautiful: the terraces there remind me of Osborne. I can see in many things where dear Papa got his ideas from for Osborne and for his decorations, which Professor Grüner understood so well to carry out.

Many thanks for your having told Lady Churchill to send me an account of your opening of the Park.* I am glad all went off so well, and that you were not the worse for it.

I have quite refused going to Naples. We shall arrange probably to go for two days to Castellamare (one hour from Naples); from thence to Sorrento and Pompeii, and return here. As yet it is not hot here at all.

Rome: April 9.

Let me thank you for your letter written on our dear Victoria's birthday. I have never been away from her on her birthday before, and though we see such fine interesting things, yet I feel very home-sick for the dear children always. In three weeks or less I shall see them all again. I look forward to the time with perfect impatience, as I am so rarely separated from them, and we live so much together. Every other day Fräulein Kitz and Orchard write, so that I have news daily.

Louis's father wrote to me to-day, as his sister asks us to her house at Sorrento for one or two nights for the 12th; but as I was rather deranged

* The opening of Victoria Park, in the East End of London, on the 2nd of April.

from a sick headache yesterday, I shall wait a day before we decide. It is wet and quite cold to-day.

We visited San Clemente two days ago, and Father Mulooly took us through the three churches —one under the other. The antique one was full of water, and we walked about on rickety planks, each with a lighted taper, as it is quite dark there. It is most curious, and the old paintings on the walls telling the legend of St. Clement are wonderfully full of expression and feeling for the time they were done.

Rome: April 19.

. . . Our visit to Sorrento went off well. We got there at one on Monday morning for luncheon. The sun had given me a dreadful headache, which ended in sickness, so that I could not leave my room. Marie sat with me, and was very dear and kind. The next day, she and my Aunt, who seems tired and dispirited, had bad headaches. We went with my father-in-law and some of the ladies and gentlemen on the following afternoon in the Empress's yacht to Capri, close by, to see the blue grotto.

The Bay of Naples, particularly seen from Sor-

rento, is most lovely—like a beautiful dream—the
colours, the outlines are so perfect.

We breakfasted together in the mornings with
Aunt and Marie, and on Tuesday we took our
leave.

We shall go to Florence the 23rd (the first station homewards); remain there three or four days;
one night at Verona, and then home. It is a fatiguing journey, and we have so often had people
in the carriage, which is very unpleasant—some
very rude English, going to Sorrento; they did not
know us.

Florence: April 25.

Your kind wishes I received early this morning.
Thousand thanks for them, and for the presents
which I shall find on getting home!

I shall be so glad to have a large photograph
of yourself. Thirty years! Good-bye, youth! but I
feel quite as old as I am, though the time has flown
by so fast. I would it had flown as well as it has
fast! I look back to the past with great gratitude
to the Almighty for innumerable blessings, and
pray our life may continue so blest. I have a very
bad headache—neuralgia; I have it continually,
and the journey is very long and tiring. Darling
Ernie wanted to buy something for my birthday,

and he thought a china doll with a bath would be the best. I am glad Victoria remembered to write to Beatrice as I told her; they are very fond of their Auntie.

Florence seems a beautiful town, and the situation amongst the hills, over which the suburbs spread, is most picturesque.

Darmstadt: June 9.

Tender thanks for your last letter, and for every word of sympathy! The weary days drag on, and bring much pain at times, though there are moments of comfort, and even consolation.

The horror of my Darling's sudden death* at times torments me too much, particularly waking of a morning; but when I think he is at rest, free from the sorrow we are suffering, and from every evil to come, I feel quite resigned. He was such a bright child. It seems so quiet next door; I miss the little feet, the coming to me, for we lived so much together, and Ernie feels so lost, poor love.

We were at the Mausoleum with all the children yesterday evening. It is a quiet spot amidst

* The allusion is to the death of the little Prince Frederick, who was killed on the 29th of the previous month by a fall from a window.

trees and flowers, with a lovely view towards the hills and plain. He loved flowers so much. I can't see one along the roadside without wishing to pick it for him.

There is a young sculptor from Stuttgart, who was accidentally here, and, meeting the children, had asked permission to make medallions of them. The *last* afternoon sweet Frittie had sat to him, and he is now making a lovely bust of him, which is getting very like.

On Wednesday my mother-in-law, with her three sons, goes to Berlin; on Thursday Uncle Adalbert* will be buried in the Dom.

We shan't be able to go to Seeheim until Saturday.

How *too kind* of you to have asked us to Osborne! How a rest and home air would have revived me—and the pleasure of seeing you again; but Louis cannot leave until after his birthday. If he did get leave, it would so throw him out before he has to command; and, having been absent this spring, he feels it an impossibility, and this I am sure you will understand. I could not leave him or the children. Our circle has grown smaller, and drawn us all the more together with a dread of

* Princess Charles's brother, Prince Adalbert of Prussia.

parting from each other. We thank you a thousand times for the kind offer.

Seeheim: June 22.

. . . I do earnestly hope that too long a time may not elapse before we meet.

It is very hot, and I feel very low and unhappy.

To-morrow this house will be full, and all the Russians, &c., close by. Had there only been any other quiet country place to be at, how gladly would I have escaped this!

. . . It is only three weeks to-day since we took our darling to his last resting-place! I wish I could go there to-day, but it is too hot and too far.

Fritz and Louise of Baden came two days ago to Darmstadt, to see my parents-in-law and us.

Dr. Macleod's letter is very kind.

I enclose two photographs of dear Frittie out of groups, the negative of one of which unluckily does not exist any more. The little blouse is the one he had on on that terrible day. My darling sweet child—to have lost him so! To my grave shall I carry this sorrow with me.

In the book you sent me there is a fine poem by Miss Procter, "Our grief, our friend," called

Friend sorrow, which expresses so much what I myself feel about a deep grief.

Seeheim: June 27.

. . . It was just four weeks yesterday since our darling died, and we went to the Mausoleum. I felt the whole weight of my sorrow, and the terrible shock doubly again. But the precious child does not—that is a comfort. He is happy and at rest, whilst we grieve and mourn. Ernie always prays for Frittie, and talks to me of him when we walk together.

Aunt Marie arrived at two on Monday, and a few hours later came to see me, and was so sympathising, motherly, and loving; it touched me much. At such moments she is peculiarly soft and womanly, and she loves her own children so tenderly. She cried much, and told me of the sad death of her eldest girl, who was seven, and of the terrible, irreparable loss her eldest son was to her. She has such a religious, truly resigned way of looking at great sorrows such as these. In the room I am now living in Aunt Marie had seen Frittie in his bath two years ago, and she remembered all about him. She is coming to "Sunshine's" toilet this evening; it always amuses her, and she is very fond of the children.

Seeheim: July 9.

. . . There are days which seem harder than others, and when I feel very heartsick, prayer and quiet and solitude do me good.

I hear Affie* comes on Thursday night. This evening the Emperor arrives. Poor Marie** is very happy, and so quiet. . . . How I feel for the parents, this only daughter (a character of *Hingebung* [perfect devotion] to those she loves), the last child entirely at home, as the parents are so much away that the two youngest, on account of their studies, no more travel about.

Seeheim: July 26.

. . . I am glad that you have a little coloured picture of my darling. I feel lower and sadder than ever, and miss him so much, so continually. There is such a gap between Ernie and Sunny, and the two boys were such a pretty pair, and were become such companions. Having so many girls, I was so proud of our two boys! The pleasure did not last long, but he is *mine* more than ever now. He seems near me always, and I carry his precious

* Duke of Edinburgh.
** The Grand Duchess Marie, who was engaged on the 11th of July to the Duke of Edinburgh.

image in my heart everywhere. That can never fade or die!

Seeheim: August 2.

Many thanks for your dear letter! I am feeling so low and weak to-day that kind words are doubly soothing. You feel so with me, when you understand how long and deep my grief must be. And does one not grow to love one's grief, as having become part of the being one loved—as if through *this* one could still pay a tribute of love to them, to make up for the terrible loss, and missing of not being able to do anything for the beloved one any more?* I am so much with my children, and am so accustomed to care for them and their wants daily, that I miss not having Frittie, the object of our greatest care, far more than words can describe; and in the quiet of our everyday life, where we have only the children around us, it is doubly

---

* How these words recall those of Constance (*King John*, act III. scene 4):—

> Grief fills the room up of my absent child,
> Lies in his bed, walks up and down with me,
> Puts on his pretty looks, repeats his words,
> Remembers me of all his gracious parts,
> Stuffs out his vacant garments with his form;
> Then have I reason to be fond of grief.

and trebly felt, and is a sorrow that has entered into the very heart of our existence.

May the hour of trial and grief bring its blessing with it, and not have come in vain! The day passes so quickly, when one can do good and make others happy, and one leaves always so much un-done. I feel more than ever, one should put no-thing off; and children grow up so quickly and leave one, and I would long that mine should take no-thing but the recollection of love and happiness from their home with them into the world's fight, knowing that they have there *always* a safe harbour, and open arms to comfort and encourage them when they are in trouble. I do hope that this may become the case, though the lesson for parents is so difficult, being continually *giving*, without always finding the return.

Dear Fanny Baillie * has been a few days here, and goes to England to-day. I shall miss her so much. I am so very fond of her. I hope you will see her; she will bring you many messages from us.

Seeheim: August 16.

. . . Louis joins with me in saying that we shall

* Lady Frances Baillie, sister of Lady Augusta Stanley and late Earl of Elgin.

gratefully accept your wish that we should come to Windsor, and he trusts there will be no difficulties for leave then. . . .

Seeheim: September 7.

. . . You ask if I can play yet? I feel as if I could not, and I have not yet done so. In my own house it seems to me, as if I never could play again on that piano, where little hands were nearly always thrust when I wanted to play. Away from home—in England—much sooner. I had played so often lately that splendid, touching funeral march of Chopin's, and I remember it is the last thing I played, and then the boys were running in the room.

Mary Teck came to see me and remained two nights, so warm-hearted and sympathising. I like to talk of him to those who love children, and can understand how great the gap, how intense the pain, the ending of a little bright existence causes.

Heiden, Appenzell: October 7.

How kind of you to remember our darling's birthday; we both thank you for this. Sad and many are our thoughts. I think of my loneliness and anxiety when he was born, with Louis far

away in the midst of danger—a sad and awful
time to come into the world; but sweet Frittie was
my comfort and occupation, a second son, a pleasure to us both! Now all this is wiped out, and
our parents' hearts are sore, and asking for the
dear bright face we miss so much from amongst
our circle of children! He ended his fight very
soon. May we all follow in a way as peaceful, with
as little struggle and pain, and leave an image of
as much love and brightness behind, to be a
blessed remembrance for the rest of our lives!

I can't write on any other subject to-day, therefore close these short lines with much love from
your devoted child,

ALICE.

Buckingham Palace: December 20.

Beloved Mama,

How much I thank you for your dear precious
letter, and for all the true love and considerate
sympathy you showed me during our visit! It has
soothed and comforted me, I assure you, and will be
a pleasure and satisfaction for me to look back to
the many pleasant talks we had together.

Louis, who has always been so devoted to you,
was touched to tears, as I was, by your expressions
of love to us and to our children.

Thank you also for all advice, which is so precious to me, and in following it I shall like to think that I am doing something that you told me.

How much I felt in parting from you I cannot say. Neither did I like to speak of it, for it was too much, and the harder things in life are better borne in silence, as none can bear them for one, and they must be fought out by oneself.

Ernie and Irène send endless loves to you, to Uncle and Auntie. Sunny's hand is better.

Tilla came to see me yesterday, and we both drove with her to the Memorial.*

. . . There is so much I would run on about, now the dear habit of intercourse together has once more become so natural to me. Writing is at best a poor *remplaçant.*

Once more from both of us warm and tender thanks for so much love and kindness! Love to Leopold and Beatrice; kind remembrances to all who surround you!

From your grateful and devoted child,

ALICE.

* To the Prince Consort in Hyde Park.

Buckingham Palace: December 21.

... It is fine and warm and still. I hope it will be so early to-morrow when we cross over. I shall telegraph how the passage has been.

Please thank Brown for his kind wishes. I am so sorry that I missed saying good-bye to several. To say the truth, I dreaded it. It is always so painful. The old Baron's * way of disappearing was almost the best.

* Baron Stockmar had such a dislike of leave-takings that he never let it be known when he was going away from the English Court. The first intimation of his intention was—that he was already gone.

1874.

Darmstadt: January 12.

. . . *How* low and miserable I am at times in these rooms, particularly when I go to bed, I cannot tell you! The impression of *all* is so vivid and heartrending. I could cry out for pain sometimes.

Till the first year is round this will often return, I know, and must be borne as part of the sorrow!

January 16.

. . . I know well what your grief and your bereavement were compared to mine; but they are such different sorrows, I don't think one can well compare them. Your life was broken—upset: altered from the very roots, through the one you lost; my life is unchanged, save in the mother's heart the blank, the pain which thousands of little things awaken—which by the world, even by the family, are scarcely felt; and this ofttimes lone-

liness of sentiment clouds one's life over with a
quiet sorrow which is felt in *everything*. . . .

Darmstadt: January 23.

On our dear Affie's [Prince Alfred's] wedding-
day, a few tender words. It must seem so strange
to you not to be near him. My thoughts are constantly with them all, and we have only the *Times'*
account, for no one writes here—they are all too
busy, and of course all news comes to you. What
has Augusta [Lady Augusta Stanley] written, and
Vicky and Bertie? Any extracts or other news-
paper accounts but what we see would be most
welcome.

We give a dinner to-night to the family and
entourage, and Russian and English legations. . . .

Louis sends you his love and warmest wishes
for yourself and the happiness of the dear pair, in
which I most earnestly join. God bless and protect
them, and may all turn out well!

Darmstadt: January 28.

. . . Dear Marie [the Duchess of Edinburgh]
seems to make the same impression on *all*. How
glad I am she is so quite what I thought and
hoped. Such a wife must make Affie happy, and
do him good, and be a great pleasure to yourself,

which I always like to think. I shall read to my
mother-in-law the letters, and show them to Bäuerlein. Both will be very grateful for being allowed
to see them.

We are going from Saturday to Monday to
Carlsruhe. The eldest girls and Bäuerlein, who is
going to take charge of them for a week, are going
with us.

. . . One day we have six degrees of heat, the
next two or four of cold; it is very unwholesome.

Carlsruhe: February 2.

I have a little time before breakfast to thank
you so very much for the enclosures, also the
Dean's [Stanley] letter through dear Beatrice. We
are most grateful for being allowed to hear these
most interesting reports. It brings everything so
much nearer. How pleasant it is to receive only
satisfactory reports! I fear Aunt Marie is far from
well. I should be very anxious, for she is like a
fading flower.

All the family, Hohenlohes and Holsteins, send
their duty. All their respective children and ours
were together yesterday afternoon. I hope not to
seem vain, if it strikes me that amongst all the
children my girls usually carry away the palm.
Victoria is in such good looks at present; they are

both natural and real children, and as such I hope
to be able to retain them long.

Sophie Weiss* came to see me yesterday. I
was very glad to be able to give her so good an
account of you, and how young you looked when I
had that great happiness of those few short days at
Windsor, which did me good in *every* respect. Old
Frau von Bunsen, now eighty-three, I went to see—
such a charming old lady, fresh in her mind, with
snow-white hair. You and Papa were the topic
she enjoyed speaking about, and our brothers and
sisters.

Darmstadt: March 11.

. . . I hope you were not the worse for all your
exertions. The *Times'* accounts are charming. Such
a warm reception must have touched Marie, and
shown how the English cling to their Sovereign and
her house.

We have cold, snow and dust, after quite warm
weather. I trust you will have sunshine to-morrow.

This last fortnight the news from Ashantee has
so absorbed our thoughts. It has been an arduous
undertaking, and one's heart warms to our dear
troops, who under all difficulties sustain their old

---

* A former Dresser of the Queen's.

name for bravery and endurance. The poor
42nd [Regiment] lost many through illness, too;
and I see they entered Coomassie playing the bag-
pipes!

Louis is just reading to me Sir Hope Grant's
book on the Indian Mutiny, which he kindly sent
me, and which is interesting and pleasant to read.

I am taking the first snowdrops to sweet Frittie's
grave. *How* the first flowers he so dearly loved
bring tears to my eyes, and recollections which
wring my heart anew! I dread these two next
months with their flowers and their birds. Good-
bye, darling Mama.

Darmstadt: April 7.

. . . Surely Marie must feel it very deeply, for
to leave so delicate and loving a mother must seem
almost wrong. How strange this side of human
nature always seems—leaving all you love most,
know best, owe all debts of gratitude to, for the
comparatively unknown! The lot of parents is indeed hard, and of such self-sacrifice.

April 11.

. . . The children are too much an object here:
they have too little to compare with; they would be
benefited by a change, seeing other things and

11*

people, else they get into a groove, which I know is
not good. They are very unspoilt in their tastes,
and simple and quiet children, which I think of the
greatest importance.

Louis Battenberg* has passed a first-rate
examination. The parents are so happy, and the
influence the good conduct and steady work of
the elder brother has on the younger is of the
greatest use, as they wish to follow him, and be
as well spoken of, and please their parents, as he
does. . . .

April 15.

My best thanks for your dear letter of the 13th.
You say rightly, what a fault it is of parents to
bring up their daughters with the main object of
marrying them. This is said to be a too prominent
feature in the modern English education of the
higher classes. . . . I want to strive to bring up
the girls without *seeking* this as the sole object for
the future—to feel they can fill up their lives so
well otherwise. . . . A marriage for the *sake* of

---

* Eldest son of Prince Alexander of Hesse and Princess
Battenberg married on the 30th of April, 1884, to Princess Victoria of Hesse, and brother to the present Prince of Bulgaria
and Prince Henry of Battenberg.

marriage is surely the greatest mistake a woman can make. . . . I know what an absorbing feeling that of devotion to one's parent is. When I was at home, it filled my whole soul. It does still in a great degree, and *Heimweh* [home-sickness] does not cease after ever so long an absence. . . .

Darmstadt: April 23.

. . . I thought so much of your remarks about daughters, &c., and do think it *so* natural and dutiful to remain with one's parent as long as one is wanted. Is it not a duty when no one else can take one's place? I should feel it so.

April 26.

I thank you most tenderly for your loving wishes for my birthday, received on getting up yesterday morning. You can understand that the day was inexpressibly sad, that the fair head missing in our circle was painfully felt, and that all these recollections caused me endless tears and heartache—though not for him, sweet precious child.

As you say, life at best is a struggle: happy those who can lie down to rest, having fought their battle well; or those who have been spared fighting it at all, and have remained pure and untouched, barely touching this earth, so mixed up with grief and sin!

Let me thank you for the charming photographs, and for the present towards the layette—a most kind assistance.

. . . We went to the Mausoleum. The children had made me wreaths to take there, and we all went together. How often and tenderly Ernie speaks of Frittie! It is very touching, and speaks of his deep and warm heart. He said the other day—for the recollection of death has left such a deep impression, and he cannot reconcile it with life, it pains him—"When I die, you must die too, and all the others; why can't all die together? I don't like to die alone, like Frittie." Poor child! the wish that *all* have, who love their own, so early expressed. . . .

May 4.

Many thanks for your last dear letter written on dear Arthur's birthday, of which, though late, I wish you joy. Such a good, steady, excellent boy as he is! What a comfort it must be to you, never to have had any cause of uneasiness or annoyance in his conduct! He is so much respected, which for one so young is doubly praiseworthy. From St. Petersburg, as from Vienna, we heard the same account of the steady line he holds to, in spite of all chaffing, &c., from others; which shows character.

My mother-in-law tells me that since Miechen has been allowed to retain her religion, this right will of course be conceded to all Princesses in future. What a good thing, for the changing I always thought too bad, and nowadays so intolerant and narrow. . . . To think of Mr. Van de Weyer also leaving this world! To you he will be a loss, and to all who knew him. Old friends are precious landmarks in the history of one's life, and not to be replaced by new ones; and it is sad, how time reduces the number as one gets on in life. How deeply you must feel this with each fresh loss! I feel much for you. . . .

Darmstadt: June 5.

Beloved Mama,

. . . The day (Whitsunday, and dear Frittie's burial-day) of Baby's* birth would have been too sad, had not the fact of its being your birthday given a double significance; but when I heard those bells, and became conscious again of everything, my feelings were deep and mingled beyond expression.

* Princess May, born on the 24th of May, 1874.

. . . With repeated tender thanks, your most
loving child,

ALICE.

June 11.

. . . Having no cow, or country place to keep
one, in this tremendous heat where one can't keep
milk, and dysentery carries off so many babies, it
would not be fair to deprive the poor little thing of
its natural and safest nourishment till the hot months
are over.

July 13.

The christening went off very well. Baby looked
really pretty for so young an individual. It was in
a large room. Marie [Duchess of Edinburgh], quite
in pink, held her godchild; and my mother-in-law,
with her best love, begs me to tell you, it had
pleased her so much that you had asked her to represent you. My three older girls looked very nice,
I thought, in lavender silk (your Christmas present).
I had the same colour, and "Sunny," in pink, was
immensely admired. She is still improving in looks
since you saw her.

I was glad it was another place, in different circumstances from the last christening. As it was, it
moved me much. The last time I heard these words

darling Frittie was with us, and now the chain has a gap!

. . . We can get nothing at Scheveningen except at exorbitant prices, so we go to that dreadful Blankenberghe—without tree or bush, nothing but a beach and sand banks.

Blankenberghe: July 24.

The sea air is doing all good, the children especially, the heat had pulled them so.

I have bathed once, and hope it will agree. . . . My cough and relaxed throat are getting better.

The rooms are small and few, but clean, and the cooking good, and we are quite satisfied. There is not a soul one knows.

Blankenberghe: August 16.

This day makes me think of our dear kind Grandmama, whose image still dwells amongst us! None who ever knew her can forget how truly loveable she was; and we grandchildren will ever retain such a bright recollection of her. So many little attentions, small souvenirs, kind letters, all tokens of affection *so* pleasing to the receivers.

Yesterday Louis saved a lady from drowning. He was bathing. The waves were high, and he heard a cry for help, and saw a bather struggling.

She had lost her footing. Her husband tried to
help her, but was exhausted and let her go; equally
so the brother-in-law, and Louis felt he was losing
his strength, but she kept her presence of mind and
floated. He let her go once till a wave brought her
near him again, and he caught her hand and brought
her in, feeling quite done himself. I was not in the
sea at the time, for the waves were so tremendous
that I lost my footing several times, and had come
out, fearing an accident. The lady is a Mrs. T. Sligo,
a Scotchwoman, and she has just written to me to
thank Louis.   He is a good swimmer, and very
strong.   The gentlemen are two grey-haired Scotch-
men.

Ella has so wonderfully improved since she has
been here. She is no more pale and languid, and
Ernie is another child also.

Luckily it has not been warm, so the air and
baths are doubly efficacious. They have done me
a world of good. I feel quite different to what I
have done ever since Sunny's birth. I believe the
sea to be the only thing for such a relaxed state,
and, being strong and healthy by nature, I can't
bear not being well and feeling so weak. Miss Graves*

---

* Governess to Princess Alice's children.

has returned, but the girls have been very good—
no trouble at all.

Kranichstein: August 26.

On dear Papa's birthday I must send you a few
lines. The past is ever bright and vivid in my
mind, though year after year intervenes. How must
it be for you, who live surrounded by such precious
recollections of the happy past!

Kranichstein: September 1.

. . . I shall get a comforter done for good Mrs.
Brown, kind old woman. I am glad she does not
forget me, and shall be pleased to do any little
thing that can give her pleasure. Will you tell her,
the plaid she made me still goes everywhere with
me? How is Mrs. Grant?

Louis is gone, and I have a good deal to do
every day. We breakfast at half-past eight, then I
have Baby and take the children out till eleven. I
then have business, Baby, and, at one, the elder
girls alternately for French reading. After luncheon
I write my letters, &c., and before five go out. In
the evenings I read, and have supper at eight with
the two ladies.

Ella is another child since she has been at the
seaside—fine colour, no longer pale and languid,

learns well, and is quite different.   Ernie the same,
bright and fresh; while before they had been looking pulled and weak, outgrowing their strength.

"Sunny" is the picture of robust health, and
sweet little "sister Maly" sits up quite alone, and is
very neat and rosy, with such quick eyes, and two
deep dimples in her cheeks—a great pet, and so
like my poor Frittie.

The return here has been very painful, and days
of great depression still come, when I am tormented
with the dreadful remembrance of the day I lost
him.   Too cruel and agonising are those thoughts.
I dwell on *his* rest and peace, and that our sufferings he cannot know.   What might not life have
brought him? Better so! but hard to say, "God's
will be done."

Kranichstein: September 15.

. . . ——'s conversion has created no smaller
sensation with us than elsewhere, and the *Times*
criticised his step so sharply.   It remains a retro-
grade movement for any Protestant, how much more
so for a man of his stamp! Quite incomprehensible
to me.

. . . This Catholic movement is *so un-English*. I
think, among those Ritualists there are *bonâ fide* Catholics who help to convert. . . .

I will send you sweet little Maly's photograph
next time. . . . Baby has a very fair skin, light-
brown hair and deep blue eyes with marked eyebrows, not much colour in her cheeks, but pink and
healthy-looking altogether.

Kranichstein: September 24.

. . . People with strong feelings and of nervous
temperament, for which one is no more responsible
than for the colour of one's eyes, have things to
fight against and to put up with, unknown to those
of quiet equable dispositions, who are free from
violent emotions, and have consequently no feeling
of nerves—still less, of irritable nerves. If I did
not control mine as much as I could, they would be
dreadful. . . . One can overcome a great deal—but
alter oneself one cannot. . . .

October 31.

. . . I always think, that in the end children
educate the parents. For their sakes there is so
much one must do: one must forget oneself, if
everything is as it ought to be. It is doubly so, if
one has the misfortune to lose a precious child.
Rückert's lovely lines are so true (after the loss of
two of his children):

Nun hat euch Gott verliehen, was wir euch wollten thun,
Wir wollten euch erziehen, und ihr erzieht uns nun.
O Kinder, ihr erziehet mit Schmerz die Eltern jetzt;
Ihr zieht an uns, und ziehet uns auf zu euch zuletzt.*

Yesterday Ernie was telling Orchard that I was
going to plant some Spanish chestnuts, and she
said, "Oh, I shall be dead and gone before they
are big; what a pity we had none sooner!" and
Ernie burst out crying and said, "No, you must not
die alone—I don't like people to die alone; we must
die all together!" He has said the same to me before, poor darling. After Lenchen's [Princess Christian's] boys were gone, and he had seen Eddy and
Georgy [sons of Prince of Wales], his own loss came
fresh upon him, and he cried for his little brother!
It is the remaining behind the loss, the missing of
the dear ones, that is the cruel thing to bear. Only
time can teach one that, and resignation to a Higher
Will. . . .

November 16.

Many thanks for your dear letter, and for the

---

* Now unto you the Lord has done what he had wished to do;
   We would have train'd you up, and now 'tis we are train'd
      by you.
   With grief and tears, O children, do you your parents train,
   And lure us on and up to you, to meet in heaven again.

advice, which, as a mark of your interest in our
children, is very precious, besides being so good!
What you mention I have never lost sight of, and
there is, as you say, nothing more injurious for children than that they should be made a fuss about. I
want to make them unselfish, unspoiled, and contented; as yet this is the case. That they take a
greater place in my life than is often the case in
our families, comes from my not being able to have
enough persons of a responsible sort to take charge
of them always; certain things remain undone from
that reason, if I do not do them, and *they* would be
the losers. I certainly do not belong by nature to
those women who are above all *wife;* but circumstances have forced me to be the mother in the real
sense, as in a private family, and I had to school
myself to it, I assure you, for many small self-
denials have been necessary. Baby-worship, or having the children indiscriminately about one, is not
at all the right thing, and a perpetual talk about
one's children makes some women intolerable. I
hope I steer clear of these faults—at least I try to
do so, for I can only agree in *every* word you say,
as does Louis, to whom I read it; and he added
when I was reading your remarks, "Das thust Du
aber nicht. Die Kinder und andere Menschen wis-
sen gar nicht, was Du für sie thust" ["But you don't

do so. Neither the children nor anybody else knows
what you do for them"]. He has often complained
that I would not have the children enough in my
room, but, being of your opinion, where it was not
necessary, I thought it better not. . . .

December 12.

I enclose a few lines to Mr. Martin.* I have
only had time to look at the preface, and am very
glad to hear that you are satisfied.

With what interest shall I read it! You will receive these lines on the 14th. Last year I had the
comfort of being near you. It did me real good
then, and I thank you again for those short and
quiet days, where the intercourse with you was so
soothing to my aching heart. There is no *Umgang*
[intercourse] I know, that gives me more happiness
than when I can be with you—above all, in quiet.
The return to the so-called world I have barely
made. Life is serious—a journey to another end.
The flowers God sends to brighten our path I take
with gratitude and enjoy; but much that was dearest, most precious, which this day *commemorates*, is
in the grave; part of my heart is there too, though

* The first volume of whose *Life of the Prince Consort* had
just been published.

their spirits, adored Papa's, live on with me, the
holiest and brightest part of life, a star to lead us,
were we but equal to following it! The older I grow
the more perfect, the more touching and good, dear
Papa's image stands before me. Such an *entire* life
for duty, so joyously and unpretendingly borne out,
remains for all times something inexpressibly fine
and grand! With it how tender, loveable, gay, he
was! I can never talk of him to others who have
not known him, without tears in my eyes—as I have
them now. He *was* and *is* my ideal. I never knew
a man fit to place beside him, or so made to be
devotedly loved and admired. . . .

December 14.

Before this day is over, I must write a few words
—my thoughts are so much with you and with the
past, the bright happy past of my childhood, where
beloved Papa was the centre of this rich and happy
existence. I have spent nearly the whole day with
the precious volume which speaks so much of you
and of him.

What a man in every sense of the word; what a
Prince he was—so entirely what the dear old Baron
[Stockmar] urged him always to be! Life with him
must have seemed to you so secure and well-guarded.
How you must have loved him! It makes one's

heart ache again and again, in reading and thinking of all dear Papa was to you, that you should have had to part from him in the heat of the day, when he was so necessary. *Ihm ist wohl* [With him it is well]. A life like his was a whole long lifetime, though only forty-two years, and he well deserved his rest!

The hour is nearing when we last held and pressed his hand in life, now thirteen years ago. How well I recollect that last sunrise, and then the dreadful night with you that followed on that too awful day! But it is not well to dwell on these things, when we have the bright sunny past to look back to. Tennyson's beautiful Dedication* expresses all one feels and would wish to say. I can only add, with a heavy-drawn sigh, "Oh, to be worthier of *such* a Father!" How far beneath him, if not always in aims, at least in their fulfilment, have I always remained!

December 17.

My best thanks for the letter of the 15th. Poor Colonel Grey's** death is shocking, and Bertie and

---

* To *The Idylls of the King*.

** Only child of Sir George Grey, and Equerry to the Prince of Wales. He died at Sandringham of inflammation of the lungs.

Alix are sure to have felt it deeply. Dear Bertie's true and constant heart suffers on such occasions, for he can be constant in friendship, and all who serve him serve him with warm attachment. I hope he won't give way to the idea of Sandringham being unlucky, though so much that has been trying and sad has happened to them there! Superstition is surely a thing to fight against; above all, with the feeling that all is in God's hands, not in ours!

How interesting the book is [*Life of the Prince Consort*]! I have finished it, and am *befriedigt* [satisfied]. It was a difficult undertaking, but Mr. Martin seems to have done it very well.

I am sure dear Osborne is charming as ever, but I can't think of that large house so empty; no children any more; it must seem so forsaken in our old wing. I have such a *Heimweh* [yearning] to see Osborne again after more than six years! . . .

1875.

[The following two letters refer to an opinion held and expressed in certain quarters, that the publication of the Prince Consort's *Life* had taken place too soon after the occurrence of many of the events which are dealt with in it.]

Darmstadt: January 3, 1875.

. . . It is touching and fine in you to allow the world to have so much insight into your private life, and allow others to have what has been only *your* property and our inheritance.

People can only be the better for reading about dear Papa, such as he was, and such as so feelingly and delicately Mr. Theodore Martin places him before them. To me the volume is inexpressibly precious, and opens a field for thought in various senses.

To this letter Her Majesty replied:—

Dearest Alice,

... Now as regards the book. If you will re-
flect a few minutes, you will see, how I owed it to
beloved Papa to let his noble character be known
and understood, as it now is, and that to wait
longer, when those who knew him best—his own
wife, and a few (very few there are) remaining
friends—were all gone, or too old, and too far removed from that time, to be able to present a really
true picture of his most ideal and remarkable character, would have been really wrong.

He must be known, for his own sake, for the
good of England and of his family, and of the
world at large. Countless people write to say, what
good it does and will do. And it is already thirteen years since he left us!

Then you must also remember, that endless false
and untrue things have been written and said about
us, public and private, and that in these days people
will write and will know: therefore the only way to
counteract this is to let the real, full truth be known,
and as much be told as can be told with prudence
and discretion, and then no harm, but good, will be
done. Nothing will help me more, than that my
people should see what I have lost! Numbers of

people we knew have had their Lives and Memoirs published, and some beautiful ones: Bunsen's, by his wife; Lord Elgin's, by his (very touching and interesting); Lord Palmerston's; &c. &c.

The Early Years volume was begun for private circulation only, and then General Grey and many of Papa's friends and advisers begged me to have it published. This was done. The work was most popular, and greatly liked. General Grey could not go on with it, and asked me to ask Sir A. Helps to continue it, and he said that he could not, but recommended Mr. Theodore Martin as one of the most eminent writers of the day, and hoped I could prevail on him to undertake this great national work. I did succeed, and he has taken seven years to prepare the whole, supplied by me with every letter and extract; and a deal of time it took, but I felt it would be a national sacred work. You must, I think, see I am right now; Papa and I too would have suffered otherwise. I think even the German side of his character will be understood.

One of the things that pleases people most is the beautiful way in which he took all good Stockmar's often very severe observations. And they also admire so much good old Stockmar's honesty, fearlessness, and are pleased to be shown what a dear warm-hearted old man he was. Your devoted Mama,

V. R.

———

January 27.

. . . My little May has such a cold, which lessens her usual smiles. She is a fine strong child, more like what Victoria was, but marked eyebrows, with the fair hair and such speaking eyes. She and Aliky are a pretty contrast!

February 14.

You say of the drains just what I have said from year to year; and this summer—if we can get away in the spring, when it is most unwholesome—what can be done is to be done, and I hope with better success than what has hitherto been attempted.

My little May cannot get rid of her cough, though she looks pink and smiling. I shall be so glad to show her to you—she is so pretty and dear.

My father-in-law has for the first time got the gout in his feet, and is so depressed. Uncle Louis suffers dreadfully from oppression at night, so that he can't remain in bed. He is a good deal aged, and stoops dreadfully. . . .

Louis gave me a dreadful fright last week by suddenly breaking through the ice, and at a very deep place. He laid his arms over the thicker ice, and managed to keep above water till some one was near enough to help him out. He said the water drew immensely, and he feared getting under the ice. The gentleman, who is very tall, lay down and stretched his arms out to Louis, another man holding the former: and so he got out without ill effects. As it was at Kranichstein, he undressed and rubbed himself before the stove in the Verwalter's [land-steward's] room; and he came home in the Verwalter's clothes, which looked very funny. . . .

I did not half thank you yesterday for our pleasant visit. I could not trust myself to speak. I felt leaving you again so much. It has been a great happiness to me, so *wohlthuend* [doing me so much good] to have been with you, and I can never express what I feel, as I would, nor how deep and tender my love and gratitude to you are! The older I grow, the more precious the *Verhältniss* [relation] to a mother becomes to me, and how doubly so to you!

Louis feels as I do; his love to you has always been as to his own mother; and my tears begin to run, when I recall your dear face and voice, which to see and hear again has seemed so natural, so as it ought to be! that it is quite difficult to accustom myself to the thought that only in memory can I enjoy them now.

How I do love you, sweet Mama! There is no sacrifice I would not make for you! and as our meetings are of late years so fleeting and far between, when they are over, I feel the separation very much. . . .

Marlborough House: June 15.

. . . God bless you, my precious Mother, watch over and guard you; and let your blessing and motherly interest accompany us and our children! Louis' tenderest love; many, many kisses from all children, and William's respectful duty!

Kranichstein: June 20.

. . . All Victoria and Ella tell me of their stay at Balmoral—the many things you gave them and their people—touches me so much: let me thank you so many times again. I feel I did not say half enough, but you know *how much* I feel it!

Our journey did very well; no one was ill, after

that dreadful storm—a piece of luck. You are now
again at Windsor. How much I think of you and
of dear Beatrice!

Kranichstein: October 7.

... To-day my eyes will not remain dry: the
recollection of five years ago, which brought us joy
and promise of more in our sweet second boy, is
painful in the extreme. The sudden ending of that
young life; the gap this has left; the recollections
that are now but to be enjoyed in silent memory,
will leave a heart-ache and a sore place, beside
where there is much happiness and cause of gratitude. The six children and we, with endless flowers
and tears, decked his little grave this morning, and
some sad lines of Byron's struck me as having much
truth in the pain of such moments—

> But when I stood beneath the fresh green tree,
> Which living waves where thou didst cease to live,
> And saw around me the wide field revive
> With fruits and fertile promise, and the Spring
> Come forth her work of gladness to contrive,
> With all her reckless birds upon the wing,
> I turn'd from all she brought, to those she could not
>   bring.*

* *Childe Harold*, canto III. stanza 30.

The weather is fine; it was much like this five years ago, but round Metz it rained. Louis was turning into quarters with his troops from a sortie, and he called the news out to the regiments as he rode along, and they gave a cheer for their little Prince!

It was a dreadful time of trial and separation for both of us, and Frittie was such a comfort and consolation to me in all my loneliness.

How sorry I am for poor Alix at this long separation!* For her sake I grieve at the impossibility of her accompanying him.

We hope to get back to our house by the 19th, though there will be an end of nice walks for the next eight months—the town grows so, and is all railroad and coal-heaps where we had our walks formerly, and the town pavement in the streets is most unpleasant walking. . . .

Schloss Kranichstein: October 16.

For your dear letter and for the enclosures I am so grateful, but distressed beyond measure at dear Fanny's [Lady Frances Baillie]. I had a long letter from her some weeks back, when she was more

* During the visit of the Prince of Wales to India.

hopeful about dear Augusta [Stanley]. This is too much sorrow for them all! Fanny I love as a sister, and dear Augusta's devotion and self-sacrifice to you, and even to us in those dreadful years, was something rare and beautiful. Her whole soul and heart were in the duty, which to her was a sacred one. The good, excellent Dean! My sympathy is so great with these three kind and good people so sorely tried. I grieve for you, too! God help them!

October 26.

How sorry I am for dear good old Mrs. Brown and for her sons!* Please say something sympathising from me; her blindness is such a trial, poor soul, at that age. How gloomily life must close for her!

* Her husband, the father of the Queen's personal attendant, John Brown, had just died. See *More Leaves from a Journal*, p. 242.

1876.

January 18, 1876.

No words can express how deep my sympathy and grief is for what our dear Augusta and the Dean * have to go through. With her warm, large heart, which ever lived and suffered for others, how great must her pain be in having to leave him! I can positively think of nothing else lately, as you know my love for Augusta, the General [her brother, General Bruce] and Fanny has always been great; and when I think back of them in former times, and in the year 1861, my heart aches and my tears flow—feeling what you and we shall lose in dear Augusta. My pity for the dear good kind Dean is so deep. I sent him a few words again to-day, in the hope he may still say a few words of love and gratitude to dear Augusta from me.

* Lady Augusta Stanley's life was at this time despaired of. She died on the 1st of March.

Darmstadt: January 22.

. . . Yesterday morning Ernie came in to me and said, "Mama, I had a beautiful dream; shall I tell you? I dreamt that I was dead and was gone up to Heaven, and there I asked God to let me have Frittie again; and he came to me and took my hand. You were in bed, and saw a great light, and were so frightened, and I said, 'It is Ernie and Frittie.' You were so astonished! The next night Frittie and I went with a great light to sisters." Is it not touching? He says such beautiful things, and has such deep poetic thought, yet with it all so full of fun and romping.

February 9.

. . . I am so sorry and shocked about excellent Mr. Harrison.* *What* a loss! He was so obliging and kind always in the many commissions for us children. Poor Kräuslach,** too—so sad! It is too grievous; how one well-known face—with its many associations—after another, is called away; and on looking back, how short a space of time they seem to have filled!

* Secretary in the office of the Privy Purse.
** The Prince Consort's head groom, who had come over with him to England.

Darmstadt: June 23.

. . . How sorry I am for good kind old Mrs. Brown!—to be blind with old age seems so hard, so cruel; but I am sure with your so loving heart you have brightened her latter years in many kind ways. It is such a pleasure to do anything for the aged; one has such a feeling of respect for those who have the experience of a long life, and are nearing the goal.

September 5.

It is long since I have felt such pain as the death (to me really sudden and unexpected, in spite of the danger inherent in her case) of my good, devoted, kind Emily* has caused me. My tears won't cease. Louis, the children, the whole household, all mourn and grieve with me. She was singularly beloved, and richly deserved to be so! Her devotion and affection to me really knew no bounds. I cannot think what it will be to miss her. I have *never* been served as she served me, and probably never shall be so again. It is a wrench that only those can estimate who knew her well— like poor Mary Hardinge. She came first in Emily's

---

* The Hon. Emily Caroline Hardinge, the Princess's Lady-in-Waiting, died in London on the 4th of September, 1876.

heart, and the loss for her is quite, QUITE irreparable!
Had I but seen dear Emily again! This sudden,
cruel sort of death shocks me so.

How I should have nursed and comforted her
had I been near her! She always wished this, and
told me she had such a fear of death. There never
breathed a more unselfish, generous, good character.

September 6.

. . . I fear you will find me so dull, tired, and
useless. I can do next to nothing of late, and must
rest so much. Poor Emily! My thoughts never leave
her. I cannot yet get accustomed to the thought of
her loss.

P.S.—Just received your dear note. The accounts
of my dear Emily's sad end have just reached me,
and I am terribly upset. You can hardly estimate
the gap, the blank she will leave—my only lady,
and in many ways *homme d'affaires*. We had been
so much together this last waiting; everything reminds me of her, and of the touching love she
bore me. Surely some years more she would have
lived.

Darling Mama, I don't think you quite know
how far from well I am, and how absurdly wanting
in strength. I only mention it, that you should

know that until the good air has set me up I am good for next to nothing; and I fear I shan't be able to come to dinner the first evenings. I hope you won't mind. I have never in my life been like this before. I live on my sofa, and in the air, and see no one, and yet go on losing strength. Of course this unexpected shock has done me harm too, and has entailed more sad things. . . .

Douglas's Hotel, Edinburgh: September 11, Sunday.

. . . I hear Ernie is still so dull and melancholy at missing me; he always feels it most, with that tender loving heart of his. God preserve and guard this to me so inexpressibly precious child! I fancy that seldom a mother and child so understood each other, and loved each other, as we two do. It requires no words; he reads in my eyes, as I do in his what is in his little heart.

It is so wonderfully still here, not a soul in the streets. The people of the house have sent up several times to inquire when and to what church I was going; so I shall go, as it seems to shock them, one's staying away. I shall see the Monument this afternoon, and go and see Holyrood again. The whole journey here brought back with the well-remembered scenery the recollection of my childhood, all the happy journeys with dear Papa and you. How the treasured remembrance, with the deep love, lives on, when all else belongs to the past!

I seem, in returning here, so near you and him and former happy years, when my home was in this beloved country. No home in the world can quite become what the home of one's parents and childhood was. There is a sacredness about it, a feeling of gratitude and love for the great mercies one had there. You, who never left country, *Geschwister* [kindred], or home, can scarcely enter into this feeling.

In the hopes of meeting you soon, kissing your dear hands, with thanks for all goodness, and many excuses for having caused so much trouble. . . .

Buckingham Palace: October 19.

I was so sad at parting with you yesterday. I could not half thank you for all your love and kindness during those weeks. But you know how deeply I feel it; how truly grateful I am to you; how happy and contented I am to be allowed to be near you as in old days. Darling Mama, once more, a thousand thanks for all and for everything!

The journey went quite well, and I am not particularly tired.

Buckingham Palace: November 19.

Thousand thanks for your dear letter received this morning! I feel leaving dear England, as always, though the pleasure of being near the dear children again is very great.

Let me thank you once more from my heart, darling Mama, for all your great kindness, and for having enabled me to do what was thought necessary and best. I return so much stronger and better than I came, in every way—refreshed by the pleasant stay in dear Balmoral with you, and then much better for the time here. I feel morally refreshed, too, with the entire change, the many interests to be met with here, which is always so beneficial, and will help me in every way when I get back to Darmstadt. All this I have to thank you for, and do so most warmly.

Louis, who, as you know, is full of love and affection for you, is very grateful for your kind words, and has likewise derived profit and enjoyment from his stay in England.

... My colour and strength have so much returned, that I do not doubt being well again this winter.

I went with Dean Stanley to see Mr. Carlyle, who was most interesting, and talked for nearly an hour. Had I had time, I would have written down

13*

the conversation. The Dean said he would try and do so.

With Louise I visited Mr. Motley also, who in his way is equally interesting, and has a great charm. . . .

Darmstadt: November 26.

Many thanks for your last letter from Balmoral, received yesterday morning! I *know* you feel leaving the dear place, but without going away there is no *Wiedersehen* [meeting again]. The happiness of our meeting with the dear children was very great on all sides—they eat me up!

They had made wreaths over the doors, and had no end of things to tell me. We arrived at three, and there was not a moment's rest till they were all in bed, and I had heard the different prayers and hymns of the six, with all the little different confidences they had to make. My heart was full of joy and gratitude at being with them once more, and I prayed God to make me fit to be their real friend and stay as long as they require me, and to have the insight into their different characters to guide them aright, and to understand their different wants and feelings. This is so difficult always.

Victoria is immensely grown, and her figure is forming. She is changing so much—beginning to

leave the child and grow into the girl. I hear she
has been good and desirous of doing what is right;
and she has more to contend with than Ella, therefore double merit in any little thing she overcomes,
and any self-sacrifice she makes.

Ernie is very well, and his birthday was a great
delight. Sweet little May is enchanting,—"my *weet
heart*," as she calls me. Aliky is very handsome
and dear.

Darmstadt: December 12.

I see this letter will just arrive on the 14th—day
never to be forgotten! How deeply it is graven in
my heart—with letters of blood; for the pain of
losing *him*, and of witnessing your grief, was as
sharp as anything any child can go through for its
beloved parents. Yet, God's mercy is to be found
through all, and one learns to say "Thy will be
done," hard though it is. . . .

1877.

Darmstadt: January 1.

. . . How beautifully Max Müller's letter* is written and expressed, and how touchingly and truly he puts the point of view on which we all should learn to stand! To become again pure as children, with a child's faith and trust—there where our human intellect will *ever* stand still!

I have been reading some of Robertson's sermons again, and I think his view of Christianity one of the truest, warmest, and most beautiful I know. . . .

Darmstadt: March 23.

Thank you so much for your dear and sympathising letter. These have been most painful—most distressing days—so harrowing.*

---

* Written after the death of his daughter.
** Illness and death of Prince Charles of Hesse, father of Prince Louis.

The recollections of 1861, of dear Frittie's death, when my dear father-in-law was so tender and kind, were painfully vivid. My mother-in-law's resignation and touching goodness, doing all that she could during the illness and since for all arrangements, is very beautiful!

The poor sons gave way to bursts of tears during those agonising hours; yet they held their father alternately with me, and were quiet and helpful for their mother and for him, just as their simple quiet natures teach them. I begged Bäuerlein to write to you meanwhile. I am feeling so exhausted, and there is so much to do, and we are always going from one house to the other.

It was heartrending from Monday morn till Tuesday eve, to see the painful alteration in the dear well-known features augmenting from hour to hour, though I believe he did not suffer latterly. He was not conscious, unless spoken to, or called very directly.

My mother-in-law never left his bedside day or night, and we were only a few hours absent on Monday night. Before we went home, she called our names distinctly to him as we kissed him, and he seemed to notice it; then she knelt down, and distinctly, but choked with tears, prayed the Lord's Prayer for him, calling him gently.

The next day at six we were there again, and
till half past six in the evening never left the bedside. She repeated occasionally, as long as she
thought he might hear, a short verse—*so* touching!
and once said, "Bist Du traurig? es is ja nicht auf
lange, dann sind wir wieder zusammen!" ["Art thou
sad? It is not for long, and then we shall be together again"] kissing and stroking his hands. It
was very distressing.

When all was over we four were close to her,
and she threw herself on him, and then clasped her
sons to her heart with words of such grief, as you
so well understand!

Early the next morning we went with her to his
room. He lay on his bed, very peaceful, in his
uniform. Louis had clasped the hands together
when he died, and I arranged flowers on the bed
and in the room round him.

There is a terrible deal to do and to arrange,
and many people come, and we are much with my
poor mother-in-law. Yesterday afternoon we went
for the last time, to see the remains of what had
been so precious. She read a *Lied* [a hymn], and
then kissed him so long, and took with us the last
look. Yesterday evening the coffin was closed in
presence of the sons.

We are going to the Rosenhöhe [the Mausoleum]

now, before going to Louis' mother, to put things straight there, and see if one can get by dear Frittie —it is *so* small.

The three brothers are dreadfully upset, but able to arrange and see after what is necessary. Aunt Marie [the Empress of Russia] wanted to come, and is in terrible distress; she loved that brother beyond anything. In her last letter to my mother-in-law she says, "Ich habe solche Sehnsucht nach dem alten Bruder" ["I have such a yearning after my old brother].

His was a singularly delicate-minded, pure, true, unselfish nature, so full of consideration for others, so kind. My tears flow incessantly, for I loved him very dearly.

My dear mother-in-law has such a broken ruined existence now—all turned round him! She knows where to find strength and comfort—it will not ´fail her. . . .

Darmstadt: June 7.

. . . We are going through a dreadful ordeal. The whole of Monday and Monday night, with a heat beyond words, dreading the worst. Now there has been a slight rally.* Whether it will continue

---

* The Grand Duke of Hesse was alarmingly ill.

to-morrow is doubtful. He is always conscious, makes his little jokes, but the pulse is very low and intermits. I was there early this morning with Louis. . . .

The questions, long discussions between Louis and some people, as to complication and difficulty of every kind that will at once fall upon us, are really dreadful, and I so unfit just now! The confusion will be dreadful. . . .

I am so dreading everything, and above all the responsibility of being the first in everything, and people are not *bienveillant.*

I shall send you news whenever I can, but I am so worn out. I shall not be able to do so much myself.

I know your thoughts and wishes are with us at so hard a time. God grant we may do all aright! . . .

Telegrams.

June 7.

Going to Seeheim, as great weakness has come on. Am much tired by all that lies before us, and not feeling well.

Seeheim: 13th.

Dear Uncle Louis is no more. We arrived too late.

Darmstadt: 6.20 o'clock, 13th.

Such press of business and decisions. Feel very tired.

15th.

We are both so over-tired; the press of business and decisions is so wearing, with the new responsibility.

18th.

Last ceremony over! All went off well, and was very moving.

ALICE.

Darmstadt: June 19.

Only two words of thanks from both of us for your kind wishes and letters! Christian and Colonel Gardiner bring you news of everything that has been and is still going on. But we are overwhelmed, over-tired, and the heat is getting very bad again.

. . . Will tell you what a very difficult position we are in. It is too dreadful to think that I am

forced to leave Louis in a few weeks under present
circumstances, but, if he wishes to keep me at all,
I must leave everything and this heat for a time.
These next weeks here will be very anxious and
difficult.   God grant we may do the right things!

June 28.

. . . To have to go away just now, when the
refreshment of family life is so doubly pleasant to
Louis after his work, I am too sorry for.   If I were
only better; if I only thought that I shall have the
chance of rest, and what is necessary to regain my
health!   Now it will be more difficult than ever,
and I see Louis has the fear, which I also have,
that I shall not hold out very long.

July 15.

. . . I leave on Tuesday, but stop on the way.
The children go direct and join me in Paris, when
we go on together on Friday or Saturday to Houlgate.   The trains don't fit, and one has some way
to drive from Trouville.

Houlgate: July 25.

. . . This place is quite charming—real country,
so green, so picturesque—a beautiful coast;   the
nicest sea-place I have been at yet.   Our house is

"wee" for so many, and the first days it was very noisy: and it was so dirty. The maids and nurses had to scrub and sweep; the one French housemaid was not up to it. All is better now, and quite comfortable enough. The air is doing me good, and the complete change. I have bathed twice, and the sea revives me.

I follow as eagerly as any in England the advance of the Russians, and with cordial dislike. *They* can never be redressers of wrongs or promoters of civilisation and Christianity. What I fear is, even if they don't take Constantinople, and make no large demands as the price of their victories now, the declaration of the independence of Bulgaria will make that country to them in future what Roumania has been for Russia now, and therefore in twenty years hence they will get all they want, unless the other Powers at this late hour can bring about a change. It is bad for England, for Austria, for Germany, if this Russian Slav element should preponderate in Europe; and the other countries must sooner or later act against this in self-preservation.

What do the friends of the "Atrocity Meetings" say now? How difficult it has been made for the Government through them, and how blind they have

been! All this must be a constant worry and anxiety
for you!

The children are so happy here—the sea does
them such good.   I am very glad I brought them.

Houlgate: July 28.

... Though we have rain off and on, still the
weather is very pleasant, and we are all of us
charmed with the place, and the beautiful, picturesque, fertile country. The life is so pleasant—
real country—which I have never yet found at any
bathing-place abroad yet. I have bathed every other
day—swim, and it does me good. I feel it already.
Ella is getting her colour back, and the little ones
look much better.

I send you the last photos done of the children;
Ella's is not favourable, nor Irène's, but all in all
they are a pretty set.   May has not such fat cheeks
in reality; still it is very dear.   The two little
girlies are so sweet, so dear, merry and nice. I
don't know which is dearest, they are both so cap-
tivating.

I have been to an old tumble-down church at
Dives—close by here—where William the Conqueror
is said to have been before starting for England.
His name and those of all his followers are in-

scribed there — names of so many families now
existing in England. It was very interesting.

August 22.

. . . How difficult it is to know one's children
well! to develop and train the characters accord-
ing to their different peculiarities and require-
ments! . . .

Darmstadt: September 9.

. . . I must tell you now, how very heartily and
enthusiastically the whole population, high and low,
received us yesterday. It was entirely spontaneous,
and, as such, of course so very pleasing. . . . I was
really touched, for it rained, and yet all were so
joyous—flags out, bells ringing, people bombarding
us with beautiful nosegays; all the schools out, even
the higher ones, the girls all dressed in white. The
Kriegerverein, Louis' old soldiers, singing, &c. In
the evening all the Gesangvereine joined together
and sang under our windows.

We are very glad to be at home again, and,
please God, with earnest will and thought for
others, we together shall in our different ways be
able to live for the good of the people entrusted
to our care! May God's blessing rest on our joint

endeavours to do the best, and may we meet with kindness and forbearance where we fall short of our duties!

Darmstadt: October 30.

. . . I had to receive sixty-five ladies—amongst them my nurses—and some doctors from here and other towns, all belonging to my Nursing Society, which has now existed ten years. Then I was at the opening of my Industrial Girls' School, where girls from all parts of the country come, and which is a great success. I started it two years ago. On Sunday I took the children to hear the Sunday school, which interested them very much.

I have been doing too much lately, though, and my nerves are beginning to feel the strain, for sleep and appetite are no longer good. Too much is demanded of one; and I have to do with so many things. It is more than my strength can stand in the long run. . . .

December 13.

For to-morrow, as ever, my tenderest sympathy! Time shows but more and more what we all lost in beloved Papa; and the older I grow, the more people I know, the more the remembrance of him shines bright as a star of purer lustre than any I have

ever known. May but a small share of his light fall
on some of us, who have remained so far beneath
him, so little worthy of such a father! We can but
admire, reverence, long to imitate, and yet not ap-
proach near to what he was!

We are going with the children to-day to Wiesbaden until Saturday; and I mean to tell Vicky that
she had better give up the hope of my being able
to come for the wedding.* I could not do it. I
only trust the why will be understood. Do write to
the dear Empress about it when next you write.
How sorry I am to be absent at a moment when,
as sister and a German Sovereign's wife, I should
be there; but the doctor would not hear of it, so I
gave it up. . . .

Darmstadt: December 21.

. . . You say all that happened after the dreadful 14th is effaced from your memory. How well I
can imagine that! I remember saying my utmost
to Sir Charles Phipps in remonstrance to your being
wished to leave Windsor—it was so cruel, so very
wrong. Uncle Leopold insisted; it all came from
him, as he was alarmed lest you should fall ill.

* Of the Princess Charlotte of Prussia with the Hereditary
Prince of Saxe-Meiningen.

How you suffered was dreadful to witness; never shall I forget what I went through for you then; it tore my heart in pieces; and my own grief was so great, too. Louis thought I would not hold to my engagement then any more—for my heart was too filled with beloved, adored Papa, and with your anguish, to have room or wish for other thoughts.

God is very merciful in letting time temper the sharpness of one's grief, and letting sorrow find its natural place in our hearts, without withdrawing us from life!

———————

1878.

Though I have no letter, and expect none at such a moment, still I must send you a few lines to tell you how constantly I think of you, and of my own beloved and adored country. The anxiety you must be going through, and the feelings you must experience, I share with my whole heart. . . .

God grant it may be possible to do the right thing, for it is late, and the complication is dreadful!

I have barely any thoughts for anything else; and the Opposition seems to me to have been more wrong in its country's interest, and to have done her a greater harm than can ever be redressed. It is a serious, awful moment for Sovereign, country, and Government; and in your position none have to go through what you have—and after all so alone!

I hope your health bears up under the anxiety.

14*

April 9.

. . . Angeli has arrived, and will begin at once. We thought Ernie and Ella—Victoria is too big, though she is the eldest and ought to be in the picture; she would be too preponderant. Angeli is quite lost in admiration of Aliky and May, who are, I must say myself, such a lovely little pair as one does not often see. He will begin our heads to-morrow. . . .

Darmstadt: November 6.

. . . I am but very middling, and leading a very quiet life, which is an absolute necessity. It is so depressing to be like this. But our home life is always pleasant—never dull, however quiet. Only a feeling of weariness and incapacity is in itself a trial.

Telegram.   November 8.

Victoria has diphtheria since this morning. The fever is high. I am so anxious.

Telegram.   November 10.

Victoria is out of danger.

Telegram.   November 12.

This night my precious Aliky has been taken ill.

Darmstadt: November 12.

This is dreadful! my sweet, precious Aliky so ill! At three this morning Orchie called me, saying she thought the child was feverish: complaining of her throat. I went over to her, looked into her throat, and there were not only spots, but a thick covering on each side of her throat of that horrid white membrane. I got the steam inhaler, with chlorate of potash for her at once, but she was very unhappy, poor little thing. We sent for the doctor, who lives close by, and who saw at once that it was a severe case. We have put her upstairs near Victoria, who is quite convalescent, and have fumigated the nursery to try and spare May and the others. It is a *terrible* anxiety; it is such an acute, and often fatal, illness. . . . Victoria has been graciously preserved; may God preserve these [the younger ones] also in His mercy! My heart is sore; and I am so anxious.

Telegram.   November 13.

Aliky tolerable. Darling May very ill; fever so high. Irène has got it too. I am miserable; such fear for the sweet little one!

On the 14th of November Prince Ernest and the Grand Duke were attacked with diphtheria, so that, up to that time, Princess Elizabeth only had escaped the infection. She was sent to her Grandmother's, Princess Charles of Hesse's palace.

Telegram.   November 15.

My precious May no better; suffers so much. I am in such horrible fear. Irène and Ernie fever less. Ernie's throat very swelled. Louis no worse; almost no spots. Aliky recovering.

Evening.

Darling May's state unchanged; heartrending. Louis' fever and illness on the increase. The others, as one could expect; all severe cases. May's most alarming.

November 16.

. . . Our sweet little one is taken. Broke it to my poor Louis this morning; he is better; Ernie very, very ill. In great anguish.

Telegram.   November 16; evening.

The pain is beyond words, but "God's will be done!" Our precious Ernie is still a source of such terrible fear. The others, though not safe, better.

Telegram.　　　　　　　　　November 17.

Ernie decidedly better; full of gratitude.

Telegram.　　　　　　　　　November 18.

My patients getting better; hope soon to have them better. Last painful parting at three o'clock.

Telegram.　　　　　　　　　November 19.

The continued suspense almost beyond endurance. Ernie thought he was going to die in the night, and was in a dreadful state for some hours. Louis very nervous, too; but they are not worse. The six cases have been one worse than the other.

Later, November 19.

Ernie had a relapse, and our fears are increased. I am in an agony between hope and fear.

November 19.

Beloved Mama,

Tender thanks for your dear, dear letter, soothing and comforting!

Our sweet May waits for us up there, and is not going through our agony, thank God! Her bright, happy, sunshiny existence has been a bright spot in our lives—but oh! how short! I don't touch on the anguish that fills me, for God in His mercy helps me, and it must be borne; but to-day, again, the fear and anxiety for Ernie is still greater. This is quite agonising to me; *how* I pray that he may be spared to me!

His voice is so thick; new membranes have appeared. He cries at times so bitterly, but he is gayer just now.

To a mother's heart, who would spare her children every pain, to have to witness what I have, and am still doing, knowing all these precious lives hanging on a thread, is an agony barely to be conceived, save by those who have gone through it.

. . . Your letter says so truly all I feel. I can but say, in all one's agony there is a mercy and a peace of God, which even now He has let me feel. . . .

P.S.—I mean to try and drive a little this afternoon. I shall go out with Orchie. Of my six children, since a week none more about me, and not my husband. It is like a very awful dream to me.

November 22.

Beloved Mama,

Many thanks for your dear letter, and for all the expressions of sympathy shown by so many! I am *very* grateful for it.

Dear Ernie having been preserved through the greatest danger is a source of such gratitude! These have been terrible days! He sent a book to May this morning. It made me almost sick to smile at the dear boy. But he must be spared yet awhile what to him will be such a sorrow.

For myself, darling Mama, God has given me comfort and help in all this trouble, and I am sure His Spirit will remain near us in the trials to come! Great sympathy, such as all show, is a balm; but I am very tired, and the pain is often very great; but pain can be turned into a blessing, and I pray this may be so. . . .

When alone, I rest; and writing even is a physical exertion. Those around me have spared me all they could, but one must bear the greater weight oneself.

May God spare you all future sorrow, and give you the peace which He alone can give!

P.S.—I finish these lines at my dear Louis' bed. He thanks you so much for your dear loving sympathy. Thank God, he is doing well. But the pain they have all gone through in their poor throats has been *awful*. The doctors and nurses—eight! for they have changed day and night, and had such constant attendance—have been *all* I could wish.

Your loving child,

ALICE.

Darmstadt: December 1.

. . . Everyone shows great sympathy, I hear, everywhere. . . . All classes have shown a great attachment to us personally, and to the House, and amongst the common people—it goes home to them that our position does not separate us so very far from them, and that in death, danger, and sorrow the palace and the hut are visited alike.

So many deep and solemn lessons one learns in these times, and I believe all works together for good for those who believe in God. . . .

December 2.

So many pangs and pains come, and must yet for years to come. Still, gratitude for those left is *so* strong, and indeed resignation entire and complete to a higher will; and so we all feel together, and encourage each other. Life is *not* endless in this world, God be praised! There is much joy— but oh! so much trial and pain; and, as the number of those one loves increases in Heaven, it makes our passage easier—and *home* is there!

Ever your loving child,

ALICE.

December 6.

Louis and Ernie will go out in a shut carriage to-day, though it rains—but it is warm. Louis' strength returns *so* slowly. Of course he shuns the return to life, where our loss will be more realised; to him, shut off so long, it is more like a dream. I am so thankful they were all spared the dreadful realities I went through — and alone. My cup seemed very full, and yet I have been enabled to bear it. But daily I must struggle and pray for resignation; it is a cruel pain, and one that will last years, as I know but too well.

Ever your loving child,

A.

A WATCHER BY THE DEAD.

A WATCHER BY THE DEAD.

[THE beautiful sketch which follows appeared in the *Darmstädter Zeitung*, dated "Chrismas Eve, 1878"; and the annexed translation of it, by Sir Theodore Martin, appeared a few days afterwards in the *Times*.]

A WATCHER BY THE DEAD.

LONG, long before daybreak on one of those gloomy December days of last week an officer made his way hurriedly along the empty, silent streets of the capital. He was in full uniform, but its pomp and splendour were shrouded in a thick covering of crape, for he was afoot thus early to do duty by the bier of the beloved Princess. Desolate were the streets, as of a city of the dead; desolate as though tenanted only by the dead was the lordly palace to which he bent his steps. The sentinels

at the great gate stood motionless, despite the
severe cold, as if they feared to disturb the repose
of death. Here, where the inhabitants of the
capital used to see all astir with the busy, cheerful
life inseparable from the residence of a reigning
Prince; here, where, in days but recently gone by,
children, blooming and beautiful, the country's pride
and the joy of their princely parents, gave anima-
tion to house and garden, all was silent and void;
a deadly blast had swept over the till now so happy
home. The country's young, idolised mother had
closed her beautiful eyes, closed them for evermore,
after doing and enduring nobly, after tasting the
bitterness of great earthly sorrow. Many long and
woeful days, many nights of even greater anguish,
had she watched, trembled, and prayed by the
couch of a husband sick unto death, and of five
children beloved past telling. The sweet, youngest
bud in the fair wreath of princely children had
been torn from her bleeding heart, and tears—
scalding tears—for the sweet little May-blossom,
which she had herself put to its last sleep under
chaplets of flowers, flowed fast, as she folded her
hands in gratitude, when the peril of death had
passed over the heads of her husband and her
other children. "Thus do we learn humility!" she
said, with quivering lip, to a lady who stood beside

her. "God has called for one life, and has given me back five for it; how, then, should I mourn?" And now, when, with fear and trembling, joy seemed about to enter once more into that heavily-stricken home, again the dark pinions of the Angel of Death were heard upon the air, and he bore away the truest of wives, the most loving of mothers, a sacrifice to duty fulfilled with the noblest forgetfulness of self. These were the thoughts with which the solitary wayfarer went upon his sorrowful way, and crossed the threshold of the chamber of death. With light step and whispered words the watchers by the dead whom he relieved withdrew.

Overwhelmed by the majesty of death, which met him here in its most sombre form, the newcomer bent his head and continued long in silent prayer. The Princess lay on a bier in the great hall on the ground floor, where she had so often sat surrounded by a radiant circle of guests. What of her was earthly, cased in a triple cerement, was covered with a pall of black velvet, which, however, was almost hid from view beneath a mass of flowers and palms. Upon the head of the coffin stood a little, simple crucifix of perfect artistic workmanship. Six torches on pedestals, hung with black, stood round the bier, shedding but a feeble glimmer through the hall, scarcely brighter, indeed, than the scanty light of the dawning winter day. From the wall opposite the coffin the youthful image of her husband, painted in happier times, looked sadly down upon the loved one lost. Directly opposite hung the picture which the Hessian Division had had painted for their much-loved leader, in remembrance of the glorious day of Gravelotte—a picture of battle and of the wild *mêlée* of slaughter in the silent chamber of death. He who now watched by the coffin had played a part in the conflict of the memorable day which the picture was meant to perpetuate, and he knew how deeply it was interwoven with the life of the Princess who lay there in her long last sleep. Her dear husband had gone to the campaign with his faithful Hessians; she knew his precious life to be in hourly danger; but her own sorrows and cares were not her first thought. Helpful, comforting, encouraging, she gave at all times to those who were left behind a brilliant example of cheerful and devoted courage; and when the wounded and sick came back from the battlefields in ever-increasing numbers, she it was who everywhere took the lead with noblest self-abnegation and practical good sense. By the beds of the sick and dying she stood like a comforting angel, and the love of the Hessian people twined the fairest of all diadems, the aureole of the heroine, round her princely brows.

This grateful love, not only of those who bore arms, but of the citizen and artisan as well, for which these things laid the foundation, was now sincerely and unconstrainedly busy beside the bier of the princely sleeper. Servants came, with loads of wreaths and bouquets, and arranged them upon the coffin. But it was not the official tributes of flowers from Court and noble, from the deputations of regiments far and near, which were laid as a mournful homage at the feet of the dead mistress, that touched most deeply the heart of him who stood there on guard. No, the tear that stole down unbidden, the little trivial gift of the poor and humble who lived far away from Court favour, had a greater value in his eyes. It was still quite early morning when, with the first glimmer of day, came an old peasant woman from the Odenwald. Advancing timidly, she laid, with a murmured prayer, a little wreath of rosemary, with a couple of small white flowers, perhaps the only ornament of her poor little room at home, as a token of grateful affection down upon the velvet pall. Then, thinking herself unnoticed, she took a rosebud from one of the splendid wreaths, and hid it under the old woollen dress. Who could interfere to balk the

impulse of genuine affection, that longed to carry
off some slight memorial with it? And now the
little flower is lying between the leaves of the old
Bible, and in days to come the matron, when she
turns the leaves of the sacred volume, will tell her
daughters and granddaughters of the noble lady,
too early snatched away from her people—of her,
who never forgot the poorest and the humblest of
them all.

Anon appeared the bearer of one of the proudest
names in Hesse, who was attached to the personal
service of the Princess. The official, stalwart bearing of the courtier was left outside, and, weeping
hot unhidden tears, he lingered long by the bier.
To what a lofty soul, to what goodness of heart,
was he saying here a bitter farewell! He was followed by two little girls, poorly but cleanly dressed,
and they, too, brought their tribute of gratitude—
two little bunches of violets. Shyly, almost frightened, and yet with childish curiosity, they drew
slowly nearer. They thought of another winter day,
some years ago. Hungry, chilled to the heart, they
were sitting in an empty attic; their parents were
dead, and they ate among strangers bread that was
hard and grudgingly given, when that great lady
appeared who was now sleeping here under the
flowers. From her, whose heart was ever yearning

to the orphan's cry, they heard again, for the first time, gentle, loving words; by her provision was quickly made for their more kindly treatment, and gratitude was rooted firmly and for ever in their young souls.

A deputation from the Court Theatre laid upon the coffin a wreath intertwined with pale pink streamers. Art, too, had come to mourn for her noblest patroness, who had been ever ready with her fine, cultivated intelligence to advance whatever was great and good. A servant brought a beautiful cross, of dark foliage with white flowers. It was the gift of the Grand Duke's mother, anxious to testify by an outward sign her love for her dead daughter. In ever-growing numbers came the mourners, all visibly oppressed by the weight of the calamity which had fallen upon the country. Countless were the gifts of love, of gratitude, of respect, which, now beautiful and costly, now slight and simple, arched ever higher and higher the hill of flowers above the coffin. The ladies of the neighbouring towns sent cushions of dark violets, with chaplets of white flowers. Two ladies deeply veiled brought branches of palm, from the dark green of which gleamed a white scroll—a poetic farewell word of deep feeling:—

A hurricane, charged with destruction,
  O palm, swept o'er thee.   The squall
Crash'd through thy leaves, and tore from thee
  The tenderest, sweetest of all.

The clouds clear'd away in the distance,
  The tempest seem'd over and past,
When forth from the firmament darted
  A lightning-bolt, fiery and fast.

It struck thee, O noble one, struck thee!
  It crush'd thee, and now thou art gone!
Farewell!   To our death-day thine image
  Still, still in our hearts shall live on.

There was a second poem, enclosed in a heart-shaped framework of leaves, which gave expression to the grief of a devoted soul for the high-hearted lady.

But now the hour was come for another to take the post of honour by the bier of the Princess. Silently and sadly the two men saluted. He that left took away with him a deep and elevating impression of the general love and respect paid by the people of Hesse to their too-early departed Princess, and the remembrance of that silent watch by the dead will remain in his memory for ever. And he who now entered on that honourable duty could chronicle proofs of genuine grief, of true reverence and love, not fewer nor less touching. Whosoever is thus bewept has secured the best and fairest memorial in the hearts of her own people for all time—"The remembrance of the just abideth in blessing."

SKETCH OF THE LIFE

OF

PRINCESS ALICE.

BY

SIR THEODORE MARTIN.

A SKETCH OF THE

LIFE OF PRINCESS ALICE.

BY SIR THEODORE MARTIN.

———

"Oh, sir, the good die first,
And those whose hearts are dry as summer dust
Burn to the socket."—*Wordsworth*.

December 14, 1878.

On the 14th of December, seventeen years ago,
a great sorrow fell upon England in the death of
the Prince Consort, who, if he did not die too soon
for his own happiness and fame, died at least, as
all now feel, too soon for England. That memorable
14th of December has again come round, and again
a great sorrow has fallen upon the country. The
Princess has been taken to her rest who watched
and soothed the Prince Consort in the last days of
his fatal illness, and who by her fortitude and noble
devotion helped materially, though then but a girl

of seventeen, to sustain and comfort the widowed
Queen in her measureless affliction. For the first
time a breach—and such a breach—has been made
in that family circle to which all who had the privi-
lege to know it looked as the happiest in England
—happiest, because mutual love and esteem bound
all its members together by ties knit in childhood
and never broken, and because the noble activity
for good which had been set before them in the
example of their parents kept their hearts fresh and
their minds ever open. She who, while yet a girl,
was called to play a woman's part by her father's
deathbed, has been the first to follow him into the
Silent Land.

No life could have opened more auspiciously
than that of the second daughter of our Royal
house.* From the first she gave great promise of

* "She is a pretty and large baby, and we think will be
la Beauté of the family."— *The Queen to King Leopold*, 9th May,
1843.

"Our little baby, whom I am really proud of, for she is so
very forward for her age, is to be called *Alice*, an old English
name; and the other names are to be *Maud* (another old English name, and the same as Matilda), and *Mary*, as she was
born on Aunt Gloucester's birthday."— *The same to the same*,
16th May, 1843.

"Our christening went off very brilliantly, and I wish you

beauty and of intelligence. The fine old English
names of Alice and Maud, selected for her by her
happy parents, seemed, as names sometimes do, to
be particularly fitted to the winning, open character of
her fair and finely-formed features, and their sound
was one pleasant in the mouths, not only of those
to whom she was known, but of the people, as she
grew up and was seen in public by the eager and
kindly eyes to whom the sight of the Royal children
has always been welcome.

When the marriage of the Princess Royal took
place in 1858, the Princess Alice was still only a
girl of fifteen; but she had already developed qualities of mind and heart of no ordinary kind. She
came by degrees to fill up in some measure the
vacancy which had been created by the removal of
her very gifted sister to Berlin. Naturally she was
drawn nearer to the Prince Consort; and the influence of his character and the teachings of his
affectionate wisdom sank deeply into her pure and
highly intellectual nature. He looked forward to
her future with the assurance that she would prove
all he could wish a daughter to be. She, on the

could have witnessed it. Nothing could be more *anständig*, and
little Alice behaved extremely well."—*The same to the same*,
6th June, 1843.

other hand, loved him with a devotion only tem-
pered by profound reverence for the great qualities
which she could then, perhaps, but dimly appreciate,
but the true extent and worth of which her own
subsequent experience and reflection taught her
more thoroughly to measure. When in later years
she spoke of the Prince, one saw that, as Ben Jon-
son said of Shakespeare, "she honoured his memory,
on this side idolatry, as much as any."

The teaching of that beloved father was put to
the proof in those sad days of patient watching
which preceded his death. Things were told at the
time of the devotion and the marvellous self-control
of the young girl, called so sternly and so suddenly
to face death in the person of a father, on whose
life that of the Queen herself seemed to depend,
and whose counsels she knew to be of inestimable
value to the nation. A few days after the Prince's
death, she was spoken of by the *Times* in these
noticeable words: "Of the devotion and strength of
mind shown by the Princess Alice all through these
trying scenes it is impossible to speak too highly.
Her Royal Highness has, indeed, felt that it was
her place to be a comfort and a support to her
mother in her affliction, and to her dutiful care we
may perhaps owe it that the Queen has borne her
loss with exemplary resignation, and a composure

which, under so sudden and terrible a bereavement, could not have been anticipated." The knowledge of this fact—and it was a fact—sank deeply into people's minds. It was never forgotten, and from that day the name of the Princess Alice has been a cherished household word to all her countrymen and women.

When, in 1862, she married the husband of her choice—a man whose sterling worth and manliness had satisfied even the critical judgment of parents jealous for the happiness of a daughter so justly dear—the affectionate good wishes of the Queen's subjects of all grades went with her to her new home. In that home, brightened and ennobled as it was by her presence, her love for the home and country of her youth burned with a steady and ever-deepening glow. It is only those who know how strong is the mutual love by which the children of Queen Victoria are bound to their parent and to each other, who can appreciate the passionate yearning towards England of the Princesses whose homes have been made elsewhere. England and all its interests held a foremost place in the heart of the Princess Alice; and no one watched more closely every phase of the changeful life of the busy land, which she loved and reverenced as the home of liberty and the pioneer of civilisation.

While fulfilling with exemplary devotion every duty as a wife and mother, the process of self-culture was never relaxed. Every refined taste was kept alive by fresh study, fresh practice, fresh observation; neither was any effort spared to keep abreast with all that the best intellects of the time were adding to the stores of invention, of discovery, of observation, and of thought. Each successive year taught her better to estimate the value of the principles in religion, in morals, and in politics in which she had been trained. As her knowledge of the world and of man grew, she could see the wide range of fact upon which they were based, and their fitness as guides amid the perplexing experiences of human life, which, however seemingly varied in different epochs, are ever essentially the same. Then the significance of the Prince Consort's habit of judging everything by some governing principle, and working always by strict method, became clear to her; and in a letter written in January 1875, of which a copy is before us, the Princess writes with her accustomed modesty: "Living with thinking and cultivated Germans, much in Papa has explained itself to me, which formerly I could less understand, or did not appreciate so much as I ought to have done."

She inherited much of her father's practical

good sense, and, like him, was ever ready to take part in any well-directed effort for raising the condition of the toilworn and the poor. How much of their misery, nay, of their evil ways, was due to their wretched habitations, she, like him, felt most keenly; and she gave her sympathy and support to every effort for their improvement. With this view she translated into German some of Miss Octavia Hill's essays *On the Homes of the London Poor*, and published them with a little preface of her own (to which only her initial A. was affixed), in the hope that the principles, which had been successfully applied in London by Miss Hill and her coadjutors, might be put into action in some of the German cities. No good work appealed to her in vain. The great exemplar of her father was always before her; and in the letter from which we have already quoted she speaks of his life "spent in the highest aims, and with the noblest conception of duty," as a "leading star" to her own.

That sense of duty carried her to the bedside of the Prince of Wales when, at the end of 1871, he was struck down at Sandringham by the fell disease under which his father had sunk. There she fulfilled the same priceless offices which she had ten years before discharged at Windsor Castle.

It pleased Heaven to spare her a renewal of the
great affliction of 1861; and in the very days of
December in which we are now living, the life of
the much-loved brother, which had been well-nigh
despaired of, came slowly back to requite her affection, and in answer to her prayers.

The trials of that time came, before the exhaustion had passed away both of body and mind which
the Princess had undergone during the Franco-
German war.   Separated—and for the second time
—by war from the Prince of Hesse, who was away
in the thickest of the perils of that campaign, she
was not a woman to give herself up to morbid
brooding on the pangs and apprehensions under
which, devoted wife as she was, she yet could not
fail to suffer most acutely, for her feelings were
warm, and her imagination active beyond that of
most women. In the hospital at Darmstadt, crowded
with the soldiers, French as well as German, who
had come from the battlefields maimed and racked
with pain, she was foremost with her bright intelligence, her helpful sympathy, and her tender hand,
in soothing pain, and inspiring that sense of manly
gratitude which is the best of panaceas to a soldier's
sick-bed.   What she was and what she did at that
time have embalmed her image in many a heart,

and will make the tears flow thick and fast in many
manly eyes at the thought of the death of one so
young, so good, so gifted, and so fair. To her it
was merely duty—duty to be done at every cost;
but how much it had cost to that finely touched
spirit and to that delicate womanly frame might be
read, by all who could look below the surface, in
the deep earnestness of her eyes and the deeper
earnestness of her thoughts. The pain of that terrible period would not let itself be forgotten even
in the gratitude which she felt for the providence
which restored her beloved husband to her side,
and for the realisation of her father's cherished
dream of an United Germany, which had been
purchased by the valour and the sufferings of its
sons.

The Princess's fortitude had already been severely
tried in the war between Prussia and Austria in
1866. Hesse-Darmstadt was engaged upon the side
of Austria, and her husband, Prince Louis, took the
field with the troops of the Principality. At the
very time his third daughter, the Princess Irène,
was born, he was with the army; and the Princess
Alice knew he was under fire but was unable to
get any tidings from him. The victorious Prussians marched into Darmstadt, while the Princess,

newly made a mother, was still confined to her
room.

Of the sad aspects of life it had been her
destiny to see much—as daughter, as sister, and as
woman. In June 1873, a terrible calamity fell upon
her as a mother. A child—one especially beloved
—climbing to an open window in a room adjoining
that in which she was, lost its balance, and was
killed almost before her eyes, as she rushed in
terror to call him back. This, too, had to be borne.
It was borne nobly, and with Christian resignation.
But such shocks tell upon the vital powers, and
some trace of what had been "undergone and overcome" seemed to be visible long afterwards in a
perceptible bodily languor, and in a more spiritual
beauty which had passed into her expressive face.

The thought of this sent an anxious thrill through
the hearts of many, when it became known that the
Princess was herself seized by the terrible malady
which had prostrated her husband and five of her
children, and taken from her the youngest of them
all—the youngest, the brightest, the idol of her other
children.* She had nursed them all through their

---

* The struggle to conceal from the other children that their
favourite was dead cost the Princess, down to the time of her

time of danger, and now, spent with watching and anxiety as she was, the malady had laid its fatal clutch upon herself. She that had cared and thought for all was soon past all human care to save. Thus she died as she had lived, devoted, self-sacrificing, purified by great pain and great love—a model daughter—wife—mother.

Of the loss of such a woman to the husband to whom she was the all-in-all, to the children to whose love she will respond no more, to the mother in whose thoughts she is interwoven with the sweetest, the saddest, the most sacred memories, to the brothers and sisters whom she loved and who loved her so truly, so tenderly, who dare trust himself to speak? It must be long before the grief can be assuaged, under which all these must now be suffering—before the "Idea of her life can sweetly creep," as something hallowed, "into their study of imagination;" but the day will come when they will bless

own fatal seizure, such a daily and almost hourly effort as, in her weak state, she was ill able to bear. Her sufferings during her short illness, which lasted less than a week, were borne with exemplary patience, and an unselfish and even cheerful spirit which were truly admirable. The day before she died, she expressed to Sir William Jenner her regret that she should cause her mother so much anxiety.

God, that theirs was a wife, a daughter, a sister, a mother, so good, so noble, and that, having fought her fight on earth valiantly, yet meekly, she has gone where there is no more sorrow, nor crying, and where the great mysteries of life alone find their solution.

THEODORE MARTIN.

————

I N D E X.

INDEX.

G

H

S

THE END.

October  1885.

TAUCHNITZ EDITION.

Each volume 1 Mark 60 Pf. or 2 Francs.

This Collection of British Authors, Tauchnitz Edition, will contain the new works of the most admired English and American Writers, immediately on their appearance, with copyright for continental circulation.

Contents:

Latest Volumes:

A Second Life. By Mrs. *Alexander*, 3 vols.

The Story of Dorothy Grape, etc. By *Johnny Ludlow*, 1 v.

Colonel Enderby's Wife. By *Lucas Malet*, 2 vols.

A Family Affair. By *Hugh Conway*, 2 vols.

General Gordon's Journals, at Kartoum, with 18 Ill., 2 v.

A Passive Crime, etc. By the Author of "Molly Bawn," 1 v.

The two Sides of the Shield. By Miss *Yonge*, 2 vols.

In the Trades, the Tropics, etc. By Lady *Brassey*, 2 v.

A Rainy June. By *Ouida*. (60 Pf.)

Alice, Grand Duchess of Hesse (with Portrait), 2 vols.

Collection of British Authors.

Rev. W. Adams: Sacred Allegories 1 v.

Miss Aguilar: Home Influence 2 v. The Mother's Recompense 2 v.

Hamilton Aïdé: Rita 1 v. Carr of Carrlyon 2 v. The Marstons 2 v. In that State of Life 1 v. Morals and Mysteries 1 v. Penruddocke 2 v. "A nine Days' Wonder" 1 v. Poet and Peer 2 v. Introduced to Society 1 v.

W. Harrison Ainsworth: Windsor Castle 1 v. Saint James's 1 v. Jack Sheppard (w. portrait) 1 v. The Lancashire Witches 2 v. The Star-Chamber 2 v. The Flitch of Bacon 1 v. The Spendthrift 1 v. Mervyn Clitheroe 2 v. Ovingdean Grange 1 v. The Constable of the Tower 1 v. The Lord Mayor of London 2 v. Cardinal Pole 2 v. John Law 2 v. The Spanish Match 2 v. The Constable de Bourbon 2 v. Old Court 2 v. Myddleton Pomfret 2 v. The South-Sea Bubble 2 v. Hilary St. Ives 2 v. Talbot Harland 1 v. Tower Hill 1 v. Boscobel; or, the Royal Oak 2 v. The Good Old Times 2 v. Merry England 2 v. The Goldsmith's Wife 2 v. Preston Fight 2 v. Chetwynd Calverley 2 v. The Leaguer of Lathom 2 v. The Fall of Somerset 2 v. Beatrice Tyldesley 2 v. Beau Nash 2 v. Stanley Brereton 2 v.

L. M. Alcott: Little Women 2 v. Little Men 1 v. An Old-Fashioned Girl 1 v.

Mrs. Alexander: A Second Life 3 v.

Alice, Grand Duchess of Hesse (with Portrait) 2 v.

"All for Greed," Author of— All for Greed 1 v. Love the Avenger 2 v.

Thomas Bailey Aldrich: Marjorie Daw and other Tales 1 v. The Stillwater Tragedy 1 v.

L. Alldridge: By Love and Law 2 v. The World she Awoke in 2 v.

F. Anstey: The Giant's Robe 2 v.

Miss Austen: Sense and Sensibility 1 v. Mansfield Park 1 v. Pride and Prejudice 1 v. Northanger Abbey, and Persuasion 1 v. Emma 1 v.

Lady Barker: Station Life in New Zealand 1 v. Station Amusements in New Zealand 1 v. A Year's Housekeeping in South Africa 1 v. Letters to Guy & A Distant Shore— Rodrigues 1 v.

Rev. R. H. Baynes: Lyra Anglicana, Hymns & Sacred Songs 1 v.

Lord Beaconsfield: *vide* Disraeli.

Averil Beaumont: Thornicroft's Model 2 v.

Currer Bell (Charlotte Brontë): Jane Eyre 2 v. Shirley 2 v. Villette 2 v. The Professor 1 v.

Ellis & Acton Bell: Wuthering Heights, and Agnes Grey 2 v.

Frank Lee Benedict: St. Simon's Niece 2 v.

Walter Besant: The Revolt of Man 1 v. The Golden Butterfly by Besant and Rice 2 v. Ready-Money Mortiboy by Besant and Rice 2 v. Dorothy Forster 2 v.

W. Black: A Daughter of Heth 2 v. In Silk Attire 2 v. The strange Adventures of a Phaeton 2 v. A Princess of Thule 2 v. Kilmeny 1 v. The Maid of Killeena 1 v. Three Feathers 2 v. Lady Silverdale's Sweetheart 1 v. Madcap Violet 2 v. Green Pastures and Piccadilly 2 v. Macleod of Dare 2 v. White Wings 2 v. Sunrise 2 v. The Beautiful Wretch 1 v. Mr. Pisistratus Brown, M.P., etc. 1 v. Shandon Bells (w. portrait) 2 v. Judith Shakespeare 2 v. The Wise Women of Inverness 1 v.

R. D. Blackmore: Alice Lorraine 2 v. Mary Anerley 3 v. Christowell 2 v. Tommy Upmore 2 v.

"Blackwood." Tales from— 1 v. *Second Series* 1 v.

Isa Blagden: The Woman I loved, and the Woman who loved me; A Tuscan Wedding 1 v.

Lady Blessington: Meredith 1 v. Strathern 2 v. Memoirs of a Femme de Chambre 1 v. Marmaduke Herbert 2 v. Country Quarters (w. portrait) 2 v.

Baroness Bloomfield: Reminiscences of Court and Diplomatic Life (w. Portrait of Her Majesty the Queen) 2 v.

The price of each volume is 1 Mark 60 Pfennige.

Miss Braddon: Lady Audley's Secret 2 v. Aurora Floyd 2 v. Eleanor's Victory 2 v. John Marchmont's Legacy 2 v. Henry Dunbar 2 v. The Doctor's Wife 2 v. Only a Clod 2 v. Sir Jasper's Tenant 2 v. The Lady's Mile 2 v. Rupert Godwin 2 v. Dead-Sea Fruit 2 v. Run to Earth 2 v. Fenton's Quest 2 v. The Lovels of Arden 2 v. Strangers and Pilgrims 2 v. Lucius Davoren 3 v. Taken at the Flood 3 v. Lost for Love 2 v. A Strange World 2 v. Hostages to Fortune 2 v. Dead Men's Shoes 2 v. Joshua Haggard's Daughter 2 v. Weavers and Weft 1 v. In Great Waters 1 v. An Open Verdict 3 v. Vixen 3 v. The Cloven Foot 3 v. The Story of Barbara 2 v. Just as I am 2 v. Asphodel 3 v. Mount Royal 2 v. The Golden Calf 2 v. Flower and Weed 1 v. Phantom Fortune 3 v. Under the Red Flag 1 v. Ishmael 3 v. Wyllard's Weird 3 v.

Lady Brassey: A Voyage in the "Sunbeam" 2 v. Sunshine and Storm in the East 2 v. In the Trades, the Tropics, and the Roaring Forties 2 v.

The Bread-Winners 1 v.

Shirley Brooks: The Silver Cord 3 v. Sooner or Later 3 v.

Miss Rhoda Broughton: Cometh up as a Flower 1 v. Not wisely, but too well 2 v. Red as a Rose is She 2 v. Tales for Christmas Eve 1 v. Nancy 2 v. Joan 2 v. Second Thoughts 2 v. Belinda 2 v.

John Brown: Rab and his Friends, and other Tales 1 v.

Eliz. Barrett Browning: A Selection from her Poetry (w. portrait) 1 v. Aurora Leigh 1 v.

Robert Browning: Poetical Works (with portrait) 4 v.

Bulwer (Lord Lytton): Pelham (with portrait) 1 v. Eugene Aram 1 v. Paul Clifford 1 v. Zanoni 1 v. The Last Days of Pompeii 1 v. The Disowned 1 v. Ernest Maltravers 1 v. Alice 1 v. Eva, and the Pilgrims of the Rhine 1 v. Devereux 1 v. Godolphin, and Falkland 1 v. Rienzi 1 v. Night and Morning 1 v. The Last of the Barons 2 v. Athens 2 v. The Poems

and Ballads of Schiller 1 v. Lucretia 2 v. Harold 2 v. King Arthur 2 v. The new Timon; St Stephen's 1 v. The Caxtons 2 v. My Novel 4 v. What will he do with it? 4 v. The Dramatic Works 2 v. A Strange Story 2 v. Caxtoniana 2 v. The Lost Tales of Miletus 1 v. Miscellaneous Prose Works 4 v. The Odes and Epodes of Horace 2 v. Kenelm Chillingly 4 v. The Coming Race 1 v. The Parisians 4 v. Pausanias 1 v.

Henry Lytton Bulwer (Lord Dalling): Historical Characters 2 v. The Life of Henry John Temple, Viscount Palmerston 3 v.

John Bunyan: The Pilgrim's Progress 1 v.

Buried Alone 1 v.

F. H. Burnett: Through one Administration 2 v.

Miss Burney: Evelina 1 v.

Robert Burns: Poetical Works (w. portrait) 1 v.

Richard F. Burton: Mecca and Medina 3 v.

Mrs. B. H. Buxton: "Jennie of 'the Prince's'" 2 v. Won! 2 v. Great Grenfell Gardens 2 v. Nell—on and off the Stage 2 v. From the Wings 2 v.

Lord Byron: Poetical Works (w. portrait) 5 v.

Cameron: Across Africa 2 v.

Thomas Carlyle: The French Revolution 3 v. Frederick the Great 13 v. Oliver Cromwell's Letters and Speeches 4 v. The Life of Friedrich Schiller 1 v.

Alaric Carr: Treherne's Temptation 2 v.

Maria Louisa Charlesworth: Oliver of the Mill 1 v.

"Chronicles of the Schönberg-Cotta Family," Author of— Chronicles of the Schönberg-Cotta Family 2 v. The Draytons and the Davenants 2 v. On Both Sides of the Sea 2 v. Winifred Bertram 1 v. Diary of Mrs. Kitty Trevylyan 1 v. The Victory of the Vanquished 1 v. The Cottage by the Cathedral 1 v. Against the Stream 2 v. The Bertram

Family 2 v. Conquering and to Conquer 1 v. Lapsed, but not Lost 1 v.

Frances Power Cobbe: Re-Echoes 1 v.

Coleridge: The Poems 1 v.

C. R. Coleridge: An English Squire 2 v.

Chas. A. Collins: A Cruise upon Wheels 2 v.

Mortimer Collins: Sweet and Twenty 2 v. A Fight with Fortune 2 v.

Wilkie Collins: After Dark 1 v. Hide and Seek 2 v. A Plot in Private Life 1 v. The Woman in White 2 v. Basil 1 v. No Name 3 v. The Dead Secret 2 v. Antonina 2 v. Armadale 3 v. The Moonstone 2 v. Man and Wife 3 v. Poor Miss Finch 2 v. Miss or Mrs.? 1 v. The New Magdalen 2 v. The Frozen Deep 1 v. The Law and the Lady 2 v. The Two Destinies 1 v. My Lady's Money & Percy and the Prophet 1 v. The Haunted Hotel 1 v. Fallen Leaves 2 v. Jezebel's Daughter 2 v. The Black Robe 2 v. Heart and Science 2 v. "I say no" 2 v.

"Cometh up as a Flower," Author of— *vide* Broughton.

Hugh Conway: Called Back 1 v. Bound Together 2 v. Dark Days 1 v. A Family Affair 2 v.

Fenimore Cooper: The Spy (w. portrait) 1 v. The two Admirals 1 v. The Jack O'Lantern 1 v.

George L. Craik: Manual of English Literature & Language 2 v.

Mrs. Craik (Miss Mulock): John Halifax, Gentleman 2 v. The Head of the Family 2 v. A Life for a Life 2 v. A Woman's Thoughts about Women 1 v. Agatha's Husband 1 v. Romantic Tales 1 v. Domestic Stories 1 v. Mistress and Maid 1 v. The Ogilvies 1 v. Lord Erlistoun 1 v. Christian's Mistake 1 v. Bread upon the Waters 1 v. A Noble Life 1 v. Olive 2 v. Two Marriages 1 v. Studies from Life 1 v. Poems 1 v. The Woman's Kingdom 2 v. The Unkind Word 2 v. A Brave Lady 2 v. Hannah 2 v. Fair France 1 v. My Mother and I 1 v. The Little Lame Prince 1 v. Sermons out of Church 1 v. The Laurel

Bush 1 v. A Legacy 2 v. Young Mrs. Jardine 2 v. His Little Mother 1 v. Plain Speaking 1 v. Miss Tommy 1 v.

Miss Georgiana Craik: Lost and Won 1 v. Faith Unwin's Ordeal 1 v. Leslie Tyrrell 1 v. Winifred's Wooing, and other Tales 1 v. Mildred 1 v. Esther Hill's Secret 2 v. Hero Trevelyan 1 v. Without Kith or Kin 2 v. Only a Butterfly 1 v. Sylvia's Choice; Theresa 2 v. Anne Warwick 1 v. Two Tales of Married Life 2 v. (Vol. I. Hard to Bear, Vol. II. *vide* M. C. Stirling.) Dorcas 2 v. Two Women 2 v.

Mrs. A. Craven: Eliane. Translated by Lady Fullerton 2 v.

F. Marion Crawford: Mr. Isaacs 1 v. Doctor Claudius 1 v. To Leeward 1 v. A Roman Singer 1 v. An American Politician 1 v. Zoroaster 1 v.

J. W. Cross: *vide* George Eliot's Life.

Miss Cummins: The Lamplighter 1 v. Mabel Vaughan 1 v. El Fureidis 1 v. Haunted Hearts 1 v.

"Daily News," War Correspondence 1877 by A. Forbes, etc. 3 v.

De-Foe: Robinson Crusoe 1 v.

Democracy. An American Novel 1 v.

Charles Dickens: The Posthumous Papers of the Pickwick Club (w. portrait) 2 v. American Notes 1 v. Oliver Twist 1 v. The Life and Adventures of Nicholas Nickleby 2 v. Sketches 1 v. The Life and Adventures of Martin Chuzzlewit 2 v. A Christmas Carol; the Chimes; the Cricket on the Hearth 1 v. Master Humphrey's Clock (Old Curiosity Shop, Barnaby Rudge, and other Tales) 3 v. Pictures from Italy 1 v. The Battle of Life; the Haunted Man 1 v. Dombey and Son 3 v. David Copperfield 3 v. Bleak House 4 v. A Child's History of England (2 v. 8° M. 2,70.) Hard Times 1 v. Little Dorrit 4 v. A Tale of two Cities 2 v. Hunted Down; The Uncommercial Traveller 1 v. Great Expectations 2 v. Christmas Stories 1 v. Our Mutual Friend 4 v. Somebody's Luggage; Mrs. Lirriper's Lodgings; Mrs. Lirriper's Legacy 1 v. Doctor Marigold's Prescriptions; Mugby Junction 1 v. No Thoroughfare 1 v. The Mystery of Edwin Drood 2 v. The Mudfog Papers 1 v. *Vide* Household Words, Novels and Tales, and John Forster.

Charles Dickens: The Letters of Charles Dickens edited by his Sister-in-law and his eldest Daughter 4 v.

B. Disraeli (Lord Beaconsfield): Coningsby 1 v. Sybil 1 v. Contarini Fleming (w. portrait) 1 v. Alroy 1 v. Tancred 2 v. Venetia 2 v. Vivian Grey 2 v. Henrietta Temple 1 v. Lothair 2 v. Endymion 2 v.

W. Hepworth Dixon: Personal History of Lord Bacon 1 v. The Holy Land, 2 v. New America 2 v. Spiritual Wives 2 v. Her Majesty's Tower 4 v. Free Russia 2 v. History of two Queens 6 v. White Conquest 2 v. Diana, Lady Lyle 2 v.

The Earl and the Doctor: South Sea Bubbles 1 v.

Mrs. Edwardes: Archie Lovell 2 v. Steven Lawrence, Yeoman 2 v. Ought we to Visit her? 2 v. A Vagabond Heroine 1 v. Leah: A Woman of Fashion 2 v. A Blue-Stocking 1 v. Jet: Her Face or Her Fortune? 1 v. Vivian the Beauty 1 v. A Ballroom Repentance 2 v.

Miss Amelia B. Edwards: Barbara's History 2 v. Miss Carew 2 v. Hand and Glove 1 v. Half a Million of Money 2 v. Debenham's Vow 2 v. In the Days of my Youth 2 v. Untrodden Peaks and unfrequented Valleys 1 v. Monsieur Maurice 1 v. Black Forest 1 v. A Poetry-Book of Elder Poets 1 v. A Thousand Miles up the Nile 2 v. A Poetry-Book of Modern Poets 1 v. Lord Brackenbury 2 v.

Miss M. Betham-Edwards: The Sylvestres 1 v. Felicia 2 v. Brother Gabriel 2 v. Forestalled 1 v. Exchange no Robbery 1 v. Disarmed 1 v. Doctor Jacob 1 v. Pearla 1 v.

Barbara Elbon: Bethesda 2 v.

George Eliot: Scenes of Clerical Life 2 v. Adam Bede 2 v. The Mill on the Floss 2 v. Silas Marner 1 v. Romola 2 v. Felix Holt 2 v. Daniel Deronda 4 v. The Lifted Veil

and Brother Jacob 1 v. Impressions of Theophrastus Such 1 v. Essays 1 v.

George Eliot's Life as related in her Letters and Journals. Arranged and edited by her Husband J. W. Cross 4 v.

Mrs. Elliot: Diary of an Idle Woman in Italy 2 v. Old Court Life in France 2 v. The Italians 2 v. The Diary of an Idle Woman in Sicily 1 v. Pictures of Old Rome 1 v. Diary of an Idle Woman in Spain 2 v. The Red Cardinal 1 v.

Essays and Reviews 1 v.

Estelle Russell 2 v.

Expiated 2 v.

G. M. Fenn: The Parson o' Dumford 2 v. The Clerk of Portwick 2 v.

Fielding: The History of Tom Jones 2 v.

Five Centuries of the English Language and Literature 1 v.

George Fleming: Kismet 1 v.

A. Forbes: My Experiences of the War between France and Germany 2 v. Soldiering and Scribbling 1 v. See also "Daily News," War Correspondence.

Mrs. Forrester: Viva 2 v. Rhona 2 v. Roy and Viola 2 v. My Lord and My Lady 2 v. I have Lived and Loved 2 v. June 2 v. Omnia Vanitas 1 v. Although he was a Lord, etc. 1 v. Corisande, etc. 1 v.

John Forster: Life of Charles Dickens 6 v. Life and Times of Oliver Goldsmith 2 v

Jessie Fothergill: The First Violin 2 v. Probation 2 v. Made or Marred and "One of Three" 1 v. Kith and Kin 2 v. Peril 2 v.

"Found Dead," Author of— *vide* James Payn.

Caroline Fox: Memories of Old Friends from her Journals, edited by Horace N. Pym 2 v.

Frank Fairlegh 2 v.

E. A. Freeman: The Growth of the English Constitution 1 v. Select Historical Essays 1 v.

Lady G. Fullerton: Ellen Middleton 1 v. Grantley Manor 1 v. Lady-Bird 2 v. Too Strange not to be True 2 v. Constance Sherwood 2 v. A stormy Life 2 v. Mrs. Gerald's Niece 2 v. The Notary's Daughter 1 v. The Lilies of the Valley 1 v. The Countess de Bonneval 1 v. Rose Leblanc 1 v. Seven Stories 1 v. The Life of Luisa de Carvajal 1 v. A Will and a Way 2 v. Eliane 2 v. (*vide* Craven). Laurentia 1 v.

Mrs. Gaskell: Mary Barton 1 v. Ruth 2 v. North and South 1 v. Lizzie Leigh 1 v. The Life of Charlotte Brontë 1 v. Lois the Witch 1 v. Sylvia's Lovers 2 v. A Dark Night's Work 1 v. Wives and Daughters 3 v. Cranford 1 v. Cousin Phillis, and other Tales 1 v.

Geraldine Hawthorne *vide* "Miss Molly."

Agnes Giberne: The Curate's Home 1 v.

Right Hon. W. E. Gladstone: Rome and the newest Fashions in Religion 1 v. Bulgarian Horrors; Russia in Turkistan 1 v. The Hellenic Factor in the Eastern Problem 1 v.

Goldsmith: Select Works: The Vicar of Wakefield; Poems; Dramas (w. portrait) 1 v.

Major-Gen. C. G. Gordon's Journals, at Kartoum. Introduction and Notes by A. E. Hake (with eighteen Illustrations) 2 v.

Mrs. Gore: Castles in the Air 1 v. The Dean's Daughter 2 v. Progress and Prejudice 2 v. Mammon 2 v. A Life's Lessons 2 v. The two Aristocracies 2 v. Heckington 2 v.

Miss Grant: Victor Lescar 2 v. The Sun-Maid 2 v. My Heart's in the Highlands 2 v. Artiste 2 v. Prince Hugo 2 v. Cara Roma 2 v.

W. A. Baillie Grohman: Tyrol and the Tyrolese 1 v.

"Guy Livingstone," Author of Guy Livingstone 1 v. Sword and Gown 1 v. Barren Honour 1 v. Border and Bastille 1 v. Maurice Dering 1 v. Sans Merci 2 v. Breaking a Butterfly 2 v. Anteros 2 v. Hagarene 2 v.

J. Habberton: Helen's Babies & Other People's Children 1 v. The Bowsham Puzzle 1 v. One Tramp; Mrs. Mayburn's Twins 1 v.

Hake: *v.* Gordon's Journals.

Mrs. S. C. Hall: Can Wrong be Right? 1 v. Marian 2 v.

Thomas Hardy: The Hand of Ethelberta 2 v. Far from the Madding Crowd 2 v. The Return of the Native 2 v. The Trumpet-Major 2 v. A Laodicean 2 v. Two on a Tower 2 v. A Pair of Blue Eyes 2 v.

Agnes Harrison: Martin's Vineyard 1 v.

Bret Harte: Prose and Poetry (Tales of the Argonauts; Spanish and American Legends; Condensed Novels; Civic and Character Sketches; Poems) 2 v. Idyls of the Foothills 1 v. Gabriel Conroy 2 v. Two Men of Sandy Bar 1 v. Thankful Blossom 1 v. The Story of a Mine 1 v. Drift from Two Shores 1 v. An Heiress of Red Dog 1 v. The Twins of Table Mountain, etc. 1 v. Jeff Briggs's Love Story, etc. 1 v. Flip, etc. 1 v. On the Frontier 1 v. By Shore and Sedge 1 v.

Sir H. Havelock, by the Rev. W. Brock, 1 v.

N. Hawthorne: The Scarlet Letter 1 v. Transformation 2 v. Passages from the English Note-Books 2 v.

"Heir of Redclyffe," Author of— *vide* Yonge.

Sir Arthur Helps: Friends in Council 2 v. Ivan de Biron 2 v.

Mrs. Hemans: The Select Poetical Works 1 v.

Mrs. Cashel Hoey: A Golden Sorrow 2 v. Out of Court 2 v.

Oliver Wendell Holmes: The Autocrat of the Breakfast-Table 1 v. The Professor at the Breakfast-Table 1 v. The Poet at the Breakfast-Table 1 v.

Household Words conducted by Ch. Dickens. 1851-56. 36 v. Novels and Tales reprinted from Household Words by Ch. Dickens. 1856-59. 11 v.

Miss Howard: One Summer 1 v. Aunt Serena 1 v. Guenn 2 v.

W. D. Howells: A Foregone Conclusion 1 v. The Lady of the Aroostook 1 v. A Modern Instance 2 v. The Undiscovered Country 1 v. Venetian Life (w. portr.) 1 v. Italian Journeys 1 v. A Chance Acquaintance 1 v. Their Wedding Journey 1 v. A Fearful Responsibility, etc. 1 v. A Woman's Reason 2 v. Dr. Breen's Practice 1 v.

Thos. Hughes: Tom Brown's School Days 1 v.

Jean Ingelow: Off the Skelligs 3 v. Poems 2 v. Fated to be Free 2 v. Sarah de Berenger 2 v. Don John 2 v.

J. H. Ingram: *vide* E. A. Poe.

Washington Irving: Sketch Book (w. portrait) 1 v. Life of Mahomet 1 v. Successors of Mahomet 1 v. Oliver Goldsmith 1 v. Chronicles of Wolfert's Roost 1 v. Life of George Washington 5 v.

Helen Jackson: Ramona 2 v.

G. P. R. James: Morley Ernstein (w. portrait) 1 v. Forest Days 1 v. The False Heir 1 v. Arabella Stuart 1 v. Rose d'Albret 1 v. Arrah Neil 1 v. Agincourt 1 v. The Smuggler 1 v. The Step-Mother 2 v. Beauchamp 1 v. Heidelberg 1 v. The Gipsy 1 v. The Castle of Ehrenstein 1 v. Darnley 1 v. Russell 2 v. The Convict 2 v. Sir Theodore Broughton 2 v.

Henry James: The American 2 v. The Europeans 1 v. Daisy Miller 1 v. Roderick Hudson 2 v. The Madonna of the Future, etc. 1 v. Eugene Pickering, etc. 1 v. Confidence 1 v. Washington Square 1 v. The Portrait of a Lady 3 v. Foreign Parts 1 v. French Poets and Novelists 1 v. The Siege of London, etc. 1 v. Portraits of Places 1 v. A Little Tour in France 1 v.

J. Cordy Jeaffreson: A Book about Doctors 2 v. A Woman in Spite of herself 2 v. The Real Lord Byron 3 v.

Mrs. Jenkin: "Who Breaks—Pays" 1 v. Skirmishing 1 v. Once and Again 2 v. Two French Marriages 2 v. Within an Ace 1 v. Jupiter's Daughters 1 v.

Edward Jenkins: Ginx's Baby; Lord Bantam 2 v.

"Jennie of 'the Prince's,'" Author of— *vide* Mrs. Buxton.

Douglas Jerrold: The History of St. Giles and St. James 2 v. Men of Character 2 v.

"John Halifax," Author of— *vide* Mrs. Craik.

"Johnny Ludlow," Author of— *vide* Mrs. Wood.

Johnson: The Lives of the English Poets 2 v.

Emily Jolly: Colonel Dacre 2 v.

"Joshua Davidson," Author of— *vide* E. Lynn Linton.

Miss Kavanagh: Nathalie 2 v. Daisy Burns 2 v. Grace Lee 2 v. Rachel Gray 1 v. Adèle 3 v. A Summer and Winter in the Two Sicilies 2 v. Seven Years 2 v. French Women of Letters 1 v. English Women of Letters 1 v. Queen Mab 2 v. Beatrice 2 v. Sybil's Second Love 2 v. Dora 2 v. Silvia 2 v. Bessie 2 v. John Dorrien 3 v. Two Lilies 2 v. Forget-me-nots 2 v.

Annie Keary: Oldbury 2 v. Castle Daly 2 v.

Elsa D'Esterre-Keeling: Three Sisters 1 v.

Kempis: *vide* Thomas a Kempis.

R. B. Kimball: Saint Leger 1 v. Romance of Student Life abroad 1 v. Undercurrents 1 v. Was he Successful? 1 v. To-Day in New-York 1 v.

A. W. Kinglake: Eothen 1 v. Invasion of the Crimea v. 1-10.

Charles Kingsley: Yeast 1 v. Westward ho! 2 v. Two Years ago 2 v. Hypatia 2 v. Alton Locke 1 v. Hereward the Wake 2 v. At Last 2 v.

Charles Kingsley: His Letters and Memories of his Life edited by his Wife 2 v.

Henry Kingsley: Ravenshoe 2 v. Austin Elliot 1 v. The Recollections of Geoffry Hamlyn 2 v. The Hillyars and the Burtons 2 v. Leighton Court 1 v. Valentin 1 v. Oakshott Castle 1 v. Reginald Hetherege 2 v. The Grange Garden 2 v.

May Laffan: Flitters, Tatters, and the Counsellor, etc. 1 v.

The price of each volume is 1 *Mark* 60 *Pfennige.*

Charles Lamb: The Essays of Elia and Eliana 1 v.

Mary Langdon: Ida May 1 v.

"Last of the Cavaliers," Author of—Last of the Cavaliers 2 v. The Gain of a Loss 2 v.

Leaves from the Journal of our Life in the Highlands from 1848 to 1861, 1 v. More Leaves from the Journal of a Life in the Highlands from 1862 to 1882, 1 v.

Holme Lee: *vide* Miss Parr.

S. Le Fanu: Uncle Silas 2 v. Guy Deverell 2 v.

Mark Lemon: Wait for the End 2 v. Loved at Last 2 v. Falkner Lyle 2 v. Leyton Hall 2 v. Golden Fetters 2 v.

Charles Lever: The O'Donoghue 1 v. The Knight of Gwynne 3 v. Arthur O'Leary 2 v. The Confessions of Harry Lorrequer 2 v. Charles O'Malley 3 v. Tom Burke of "Ours" 3 v. Jack Hinton 2 v. The Daltons 4 v. The Dodd Family abroad 3 v. The Martins of Cro' Martin 3 v. The Fortunes of Glencore 2 v. Roland Cashel 3 v. Davenport Dunn 3 v. Con Cregan 2 v. One of Them 2 v. Maurice Tiernay 2 v. Sir Jasper Carew 2 v. Barrington 2 v. A Day's Ride: a Life's Romance 2 v. Luttrell of Arran 2 v. Tony Butler 2 v. Sir Brook Fosshrooke 2 v. The Bramleighs of Bishop's Folly 2 v. A Rent in a Cloud 1 v. That Boy of Norcott's 1 v. St. Patrick's Eve : Paul Gosslett's Confessions 1 v. Lord Kilgobbin 2 v.

G. H. Lewes: Ranthorpe 1 v. Physiology of Common Life 2 v. On Actors and the Art of Acting 1 v.

E. Lynn Linton: Joshua Davidson 1 v. Patricia Kemball 2 v. The Atonement of Leam Dundas 2 v. The World well Lost 2 v. Under which Lord? 2 v. With a Silken Thread etc. 1 v. Todhunters' at Loanin' Head etc. 1 v. "My Love!" 2 v. The Girl of the Period, etc. 1 v. Ione 2 v.

Laurence W. M. Lockhart: Mine is Thine 2 v.

Longfellow: Poetical Works (w. portrait) 3 v. The Divine Comedy of Dante Alighieri 3 v. The New-England Tragedies 1 v. The Divine Tragedy 1 v. Three Books of Song 1 v. The Masque of Pandora 1 v.

M. Lonsdale: Sister Dora 1 v.

A Lost Battle 2 v.

Lutfullah: Autobiography of Lutfullah, by Eastwick 1 v.

Lord Lytton: *vide* Bulwer.

Robert Lord Lytton (Owen Meredith): Poems 2 v. Fables in Song 2 v.

Lord Macaulay: History of England (w. portrait) 10 v. Critical and Historical Essays 5 v. Lays of Ancient Rome 1 v. Speeches 2 v. Biographical Essays 1 v. William Pitt, Atterbury 1 v. (See also Trevelyan).

Justin M°Carthy: Waterdale Neighbours 2 v. Lady Disdain 2 v. Miss Misanthrope 2 v. A History of our own Times 5 v. Donna Quixote 2 v. A short History of our own Times 2 v. A History of the Four Georges vol. 1.

George MacDonald: Alec Forbes of Howglen 2 v. Annals of a Quiet Neighbourhood 2 v. David Elginbrod 2 v. The Vicar's Daughter 2 v. Malcolm 2 v. St. George and St. Michael 2 v. The Marquis of Lossie 2 v. Sir Gibbie 2 v. Mary Marston 2 v. The Gifts of the Child Christ, etc. 1 v. The Princess and Curdie 1 v.

Mrs. Mackarness: Sunbeam Stories 1 v. A Peerless Wife 2 v. A Mingled Yarn 2 v.

Charles McKnight: Old Fort Duquesne 2 v.

Norman Macleod: The old Lieutenant and his Son 1 v.

Mrs. Macquoid: Patty 2 v. Miriam's Marriage 2 v. Pictures across the Channel 2 v. Too Soon 1 v. My Story 2 v. Diane 2 v. Beside the River 2 v. A Faithful Lover 2 v.

"Mademoiselle Mori," Author of— Mademoiselle Mori 2 v. Denise 1 v. Madame Fontenoy 1 v. On the Edge of the Storm 1 v. The Atelier du Lys 2 v. In the Olden Time 2 v.

Lord Mahon: *vide* Stanhope.

E. S. Maine: Scarscliff Rocks 2 v.

Lucas Malet: Colonel Enderby's Wife 2 v.

Lord Malmesbury: Memoirs of an Ex-Minister 3 v.

R. Blachford Mansfield: The Log of the Water Lily 1 v.

Mark Twain: The Adventures of Tom Sawyer 1 v. The Innocents Abroad; or, the New Pilgrims' Progress 2 v. A Tramp Abroad 2 v. "Roughing it" 1 v. The Innocents at Home 1 v. The Prince and the Pauper 2 v. The Stolen White Elephant, etc. 1 v. Life on the Mississippi 2 v. Sketches 1 v. The Adventures of Huckleberry Finn 2 v. Marmorne 1 v.

Capt. Marryat: Jacob Faithful (w. portrait) 1 v. Percival Keene 1 v. Peter Simple 1 v. Japhet 1 v. Monsieur Violet 1 v. The Settlers 1 v. The Mission 1 v. The Privateer's-Man 1 v. The Children of the New-Forest 1 v. Valerie 1 v. Mr. Midshipman Easy 1 v. The King's Own 1 v.

Florence Marryat: Love's Conflict 2 v. For Ever and Ever 2 v. The Confessions of Gerald Estcourt 2 v. Nelly Brooke 2 v. Véronique 2 v. Petronel 2 v. Her Lord and Master 2 v. The Prey of the Gods 1 v. Life of Captain Marryat 1 v. Mad Dumaresq 2 v. No Intentions 2 v. Fighting the Air 2 v. A Star and a Heart 1 v. The Poison of Asps 1 v. A Lucky Disappointment 1 v. My own Child 2 v. Her Father's Name 2 v. A Harvest of Wild Oats 2 v. A Little Stepson 1 v. Written in Fire 2 v. Her World against a Lie 2 v. A Broken Blossom 2 v. The Root of all Evil 2 v. The Fair-haired Alda 2 v. With Cupid's Eyes 2 v. My Sister the Actress 2 v. Phyllida 2 v. How They Loved Him 2 v. Facing the Footlights (w. portrait) 2 v. A Moment of Madness 1 v. The Ghost of Charlotte Cray, etc. 1 v. Peeress and Player 2 v. Under the Lilies and Roses 2 v. The Heart of Jane Warner 2 v.

Mrs. Marsh: Ravenscliffe 2 v. Emilia Wyndham 2 v. Castle Avon 2 v. Aubrey 2 v. The Heiress of Haughton 2 v. Evelyn Marston 2 v. The Rose of Ashurst 2 v.

Emma Marshall: Mrs. Mainwaring's Journal 1 v. Benvenuta 1 v. Lady Alice 1 v. Dayspring 1 v. Life's Aftermath 1 v. In the East Country 1 v.

H. Mathers: "Cherry Ripe!" 2 v. "Land o' the Leal" 1 v. My Lady Green Sleeves 2 v. As he comes up the Stair, etc. 1 v. Sam's Sweetheart 2 v. Eyre's Acquittal 2 v. Found Out 1 v.

"Mehalah," Author of— Mehalah 1 v. John Herring 2 v.

Whyte Melville: Kate Coventry 1 v. Holmby House 2 v. Digby Grand 1 v. Good for Nothing 2 v. The Queen's Maries 2 v. The Gladiators 2 v. The Brookes of Bridlemere 2 v. Cerise 2 v. The Interpreter 2 v. The White Rose 2 v. M. or N. 1 v. Contraband; or A Losing Hazard 1 v. Sarchedon 2 v. Uncle John 2 v. Katerfelto 1 v. Sister Louise 1 v. Rosine 1 v. Roy's Wife 2 v. Black but Comely 2 v. Riding Recollections 1 v.

George Meredith: The Ordeal of Feverel 2 v. Beauchamp's Career 2 v. The Tragic Comedians 1 v.

Owen Meredith: *vide* Robert Lord Lytton.

Milton: Poetical Works 1 v.

"Miss Molly," Author of— Geraldine Hawthorne 1 v.

"Molly Bawn," Author of— Molly Bawn 2 v. Mrs. Geoffrey 2 v. Faith and Unfaith 2 v. Portia 2 v. Loÿs, Lord Berresford, etc. 1 v. Her First Appearance, etc. 1 v. Phyllis 2 v. Rossmoyne 2 v. Doris 2 v. A Maiden all Forlorn, etc. 1 v. A Passive Crime 1 v.

Miss Florence Montgomery: Misunderstood 1 v. Thrown Together 2 v. Thwarted 1 v. Wild Mike 1 v. Seaforth 2 v. The Blue Veil 1 v.

Moore: Poetical Works (w. portrait) 5 v.

Lady Morgan's Memoirs 3 v.

Henry Morley: Of English Literature in the Reign of Victoria. With Facsimiles of the Signatures of Authors in the Tauchnitz Edition [v. 2000].

The price of each volume is 1 Mark 60 Pfennige.

E. C. Grenville-Murray: The Member for Paris 2 v. Young Brown 2 v. The Boudoir Cabal 3 v. French Pictures in English Chalk (1st Series) 2v. The Russians of To-day 1 v. French Pictures in English Chalk (2nd Series) 2 v. Strange Tales 1 v. That Artful Vicar 2 v. Six Months in the Ranks 1 v. People I have met 1 v.

"My little Lady," Author of— *vide* E. Frances Poynter.

New Testament [v. 1000].

Mrs. Newby: Common Sense 2 v.

Dr. J. H. Newman: Callista 1 v.

"Nina Balatka," Author of— *vide* Anthony Trollope.

"No Church," Author of—No Church 2 v. Owen:—a Waif 2 v.

Lady Augusta Noel: From Generation to Generation 1 v.

Hon. Mrs. Norton: Stuart of Dunleath 2 v. Lost and Saved 2 v. Old Sir Douglas 2 v.

Novels and Tales *vide* Household Words.

Not Easily Jealous 2 v.

L. Oliphant: Altiora Peto 2 v.

Mrs. Oliphant: Passages in the Life of Mrs. Margaret Maitland of Sunnyside 1 v. The Last of the Mortimers 2 v. Agnes 2 v. Madonna Mary 2 v. The Minister's Wife 2 v. The Rector, and the Doctor's Family 1 v. Salem Chapel 2 v. The Perpetual Curate 2 v. Miss Marjoribanks 2 v. Ombra 2 v. Memoir of Count de Montalembert 2 v. May 2 v. Innocent 2 v. For Love and Life 2 v. A Rose in June 1 v. The Story of Valentine and his Brother 2 v. Whiteladies 2 v. The Curate in Charge 1 v. Phœbe, Junior 2 v. Mrs. Arthur 2 v. Carità 2 v. Young Musgrave 2 v. The Primrose Path 2 v. Within the Precincts 3 v. The greatest Heiress in England 2 v. He that will not when he may 2 v. Harry Joscelyn 2 v. In Trust 2 v. It was a Lover and his Lass 3 v. The Ladies Lindores 3 v. Hester 3 v. The Wizard's Son 3 v.

Ossian: Poems 1 v.

Ouida: Idalia 2 v. Tricotrin 2 v. Puck 2 v. Chandos 2 v. Strathmore 2 v. Under two Flags 2 v. Folle-Farine 2 v. A Leaf in the Storm; A Dog of Flanders and other Stories 1 v. Cecil Castlemaine's Gage 1 v. Madame la Marquise 1 v. Pascarèl 2 v. Held in Bondage 2 v. Two little Wooden Shoes 1 v. Signa (w. portrait) 3 v. In a Winter City 1 v. Ariadnê 2 v. Friendship 2 v. Moths 3 v. Pipistrello 1 v. A Village Commune 2 v. In Maremma 3 v. Bimbi 1 v. Wanda 3 v. Frescoes, etc. 1 v. Princess Napraxine 3 v. A Rainy June (60 Pf.).

Miss Parr (Holme Lee): Basil Godfrey's Caprice 2 v. For Richer, for Poorer 2 v. The Beautiful Miss Barrington 2 v. Her Title of Honour 1 v. Echoes of a Famous Year 1 v. Katherine's Trial 1 v. Bessie Fairfax 2 v. Ben Milner's Wooing 1 v. Straightforward 2 v. Mrs. Denys of Cote 2 v. A Poor Squire 1 v.

Mrs. Parr: Dorothy Fox 1 v. The Prescotts of Pamphillon 2 v. Gosau Smithy 1 v. Robin 2 v.

"Paul Ferroll," Author of— Paul Ferroll 1 v. Year after Year 1 v. Why Paul Ferroll killed his Wife 1 v.

James Payn: Found Dead 1 v. Gwendoline's Harvest 1 v. Like Father, like Son 2 v. Not Wooed, but Won 2 v. Cecil's Tryst 1 v. A Woman's Vengeance 2 v. Murphy's Master 1 v. In the Heart of a Hill 1 v. At Her Mercy 2 v. The Best of Husbands 2 v. Walter's Word 2 v. Halves 2 v. Fallen Fortunes 2 v. What He cost Her 2 v. By Proxy 2 v. Less Black than we're Painted 2 v. Under one Roof 2 v. High Spirits 1 v. High Spirits (Second Series) 1 v. A Confidential Agent 2 v. From Exile 2 v. A Grape from a Thorn 2 v. Some Private Views 1 v. For Cash Only 2 v. Kit: A Memory 2 v. The Canon's Ward 2 v. Some Literary Recollections 1 v. The Talk of the Town 1 v.

Miss Fr. M. Peard: One Year 2 v. The Rose-Garden 1 v. Unawares 1 v. Thorpe Regis 1 v. A Winter Story 1 v. A Madrigal 1 v. Cartouche

1 v. Mother Molly 1 v. Schloss and Town 2 v. Contradictions 2 v. Near Neighbours 1 v.

Bishop Percy: Reliques of Ancient English Poetry 3 v.

E. A. Poe: Poems and Essays. Edited with a new Memoir by John H. Ingram 1 v. Tales. Edited by John H. Ingram 1 v.

Pope: Select Poetical Works (w. portrait) 1 v.

E. Frances Poynter: My little Lady 2 v. Ersilia 2 v. Among the Hills 1 v. Madame de Presnel 1 v.

Mrs. Campbell Praed: Zéro 1 v. Affinities 1 v.

Mrs. E. Prentiss: Stepping Heavenward 1 v.

The Prince Consort's Speeches and Addresses 1 v.

Horace N. Pym: *vide* C. Fox.

W. F. Rae: Westward by Rail 1 v.

Charles Reade: "It is never too late to mend" 2 v. "Love me little love me long" 1 v. The Cloister and the Hearth 2 v. Hard Cash 3 v. Put Yourself in his Place 2 v. A Terrible Temptation 2 v. Peg Woffington 1 v. Christie Johnstone 1 v. A Simpleton 2 v. The Wandering Heir 1 v. A Woman-Hater 2 v. Readiana 1 v. Singleheart and Doubleface 1 v.

"Recommended to Mercy," Author of—Recommended to Mercy 2 v. Zoe's 'Brand' 2 v.

James Rice: *vide* W. Besant.

Alfred Bate Richards: So very Human 3 v.

Richardson: Clarissa Harlowe 4 v.

Mrs. Riddell (F. G. Trafford): George Geith of Fen Court 2 v. Maxwell Drewitt 2 v. The Race for Wealth 2 v. Far above Rubies 2 v. The Earl's Promise 2 v. Mortomley's Estate 2 v.

Rev. W. Robertson: Sermons 4 v.

Charles H. Ross: The Pretty Widow 1 v. A London Romance 2 v.

Dante Gabriel Rossetti: Poems 1 v. Ballads and Sonnets 1 v.

J. Ruffini: Lavinia 2 v. Doctor Antonio 1 v. Lorenzo Benoni 1 v. Vincenzo 2 v. A Quiet Nook 1 v. The Paragreens on a Visit to Paris 1 v. Carlino and other Stories 1 v.

W. Clark Russell: A Sailor's Sweetheart 2 v. The "Lady Maud" 2 v. A Sea Queen 2 v.

G. A. Sala: The Seven Sons of Mammon 2 v.

John Saunders: Israel Mort, Overman 2 v. The Shipowner's Daughter 2 v. A Noble Wife 2 v.

Katherine Saunders: Joan Merryweather and other Tales 1 v. Gideon's Rock 1 v. The High Mills 2 v. Sebastian 1 v.

Sir Walter Scott: Waverley (w. portrait) 1 v. The Antiquary 1 v. Ivanhoe 1 v. Kenilworth 1 v. Quentin Durward 1 v. Old Mortality 1 v. Guy Mannering 1 v. Rob Roy 1 v. The Pirate 1 v. The Fortunes of Nigel 1 v. The Black Dwarf; A Legend of Montrose 1 v. The Bride of Lammermoor 1 v. The Heart of Mid-Lothian 2 v. The Monastery 1 v. The Abbot 1 v. Peveril of the Peak 2 v. The Poetical Works 2 v. Woodstock 1 v. The Fair Maid of Perth 1 v. Anne of Geierstein 1 v.

Professor Seeley: Life and Times of Stein 4 v. The Expansion of England 1 v.

Miss Sewell: Amy Herbert 2 v. Ursula 2 v. A Glimpse of the World 2 v. The Journal of a Home Life 2 v. After Life 2 v. The Experience of Life; or, Aunt Sarah 2 v.

Shakespeare: Plays and Poems (with portrait) *(Second Edition)* compl. 7 v.

Shakespeare's Plays may also be had in 37 numbers, at M. 0,30. each number.

Doubtful Plays 1 v.

Shelley: A Selection from his Poems 1 v.

Nathan Sheppard: Shut up in Paris *(Second Edition, enlarged)* 1 v.

Sheridan: Dramatic Works 1 v.

J. Henry Shorthouse: John Inglesant 2 v.

Smollett: The Adventures of Roderick Random 1 v. The Expedition of Humphry Clinker 1 v. The Adventures of Peregrine Pickle 2 v.

Society in London. By a Foreign Resident 1 v.

Earl Stanhope (Lord Mahon): History of England 7 v. The Reign of Queen Anne 2 v.

Sterne: The Life and Opinions of Tristram Shandy 1 v. A Sentimental Journey (w. portrait) 1 v

Robert Louis Stevenson: Treasure Island 1 v.

"Still Waters," Author of— Still Waters 1 v. Dorothy 1 v. De Cressy 1 v. Uncle Ralph 1 v. Maiden Sisters 1 v. Martha Brown 1 v. Vanessa 1 v.

M. C. Stirling: Two Tales of Married Life 2 v. Vol. II, A True Man, Vol. I. *vide* G. M. Craik.

"The Story of Elizabeth," Author of—*v.* Miss Thackeray.

Mrs. H. Beecher Stowe: Uncle Tom's Cabin (w. portrait) 2 v. A Key to Uncle Tom's Cabin 2 v. Dred 2 v. The Minister's Wooing 1 v. Oldtown Folks 2 v.

"Sunbeam Stories," Author of— *vide* Mackarness.

Swift: Gulliver's Travels 1 v.

J. A. Symonds: Sketches in Italy 1 v. New Italian Sketches 1 v.

Baroness Tautphoeus: Cyrilla 2 v. The Initials 2 v. Quits 2 v. At Odds 2 v.

Colonel Meadows Taylor: Tara: a Mahratta Tale 3 v.

Templeton: Diary & Notes 1 v.

Lord Tennyson: Poetical Works 7 v. Queen Mary 1 v. Harold 1 v. Ballads and other Poems 1 v. Becket; The Cup; The Falcon 1 v.

W. M. Thackeray: Vanity Fair 3 v. The History of Pendennis 3 v. Miscellanies 8 v. The History of Henry Esmond 2 v. The English Humourists 1 v. The Newcomes 4 v. The Virginians 4 v. The Four Georges; Lovel the Widower 1 v. The Adventures of Philip 2 v. Denis Duval 1 v. Roundabout Papers 2 v. Catherine 1 v. The Irish Sketch Book 2 v. The Paris Sketch Book (w. portrait) 2 v.

Miss Thackeray: The Story of Elizabeth 1 v. The Village on the Cliff 1 v. Old Kensington 2 v. Bluebeard's Keys 1 v. Five Old Friends 1 v. Miss Angel 1 v. Out of the World 1 v. Fulham Lawn 1 v. From an Island 1 v. Da Capo 1 v. Madame de Sévigné 1 v. A Book of Sibyls 1 v.

Thomas a Kempis: The Imitation of Christ 1 v.

A. Thomas: Denis Donne 2 v. On Guard 2 v. Walter Goring 2 v. Played out 2 v. Called to Account 2 v. Only Herself 2 v. A narrow Escape 2 v.

Thomson: Poetical Works (with portrait) 1 v.

F. G. Trafford: *vide* Mrs. Riddell.

G. O. Trevelyan: The Life and Letters of Lord Macaulay (w. portrait) 4 v. Selections from the Writings of Lord Macaulay 2 v.

Trois-Etoiles: *vide* Murray.

Anthony Trollope: Doctor Thorne 2 v The Bertrams 2 v. The Warden 1 v. Barchester Towers 2 v. Castle Richmond 2 v. The West Indies 1 v. Framley Parsonage 2 v. North America 3 v. Orley Farm 3 v. Rachel Ray 2 v. The Small House at Allington 3 v. Can you forgive her? 3 v. The Belton Estate 2 v. Nina Balatka 1 v. The Last Chronicle of Barset 3 v. The Claverings 2 v. Phineas Finn 3 v. He knew he was Right 3 v. The Vicar of Bullhampton 2 v. Sir Harry Hotspur of Humblethwaite 1 v. Ralph the Heir 2 v. The Golden Lion of Granpere 1 v. Australia and New Zealand 3 v. Lady Anna 2 v. Harry Heathcote of Gangoil 1 v. The Way we live now 4 v. The Prime Minister 4 v. The American Senator 3 v. South Africa 2 v. Is he Popenjoy? 3 v. An Eye for an Eye 1 v. John Caldigate 3 v. Cousin Henry 1 v. The Duke's Children 3 v. Dr. Wortle's School 1 v. Ayala's Angel 3 v. The Fixed Period 1 v. Marion Fay 2 v. Kept in the Dark 1 v. Frau Frohmann, etc. 1 v. Alice Dugdale, etc. 1 v. La Mère Bauche, etc. 1 v. The Mistletoe Bough, etc. 1 v. An Autobiography 1 v. An Old Man's Love 1 v.

T. Adolphus Trollope: The Garstangs of Garstang Grange 2 v. A Siren 2 v.

The Two Cosmos 1 v.

"Vèra," Author of— Vèra 1 v. The Hôtel du Petit St. Jean 1 v. Blue Roses 2 v. Within Sound of the Sea 2 v. The Maritime Alps and their Seaboard 2 v.

Victoria R. I.: *vide* Leaves.

Virginia 1 v.

L. B. Walford: Mr. Smith 2 v. Pauline 2 v. Cousins 2 v. Troublesome Daughters 2 v.

Mackenzie Wallace: Russia 3 v.

Eliot Warburton: The Crescent and the Cross 2 v. Darien 2 v.

S. Warren: Passages from the Diary of a late Physician 2 v. Ten Thousand a-Year 3 v. Now and Then 1 v. The Lily and the Bee 1 v.

"Waterdale Neighbours," Author of— *vide* Justin McCarthy.

Miss Wetherell: The wide, wide World 1 v. Queechy 2 v. The Hills of the Shatemuc 2 v. Say and Seal 2 v. The Old Helmet 2 v.

A Whim and its Consequences 1 v.

W. White: Holidays in Tyrol 1 v.

"Who Breaks—Pays," Author of— *vide* Mrs. Jenkin.

J. S. Winter: Regimental Legends 1 v.

Mrs. Henry Wood: East Lynne 3 v. The Channings 2 v. Mrs. Halliburton's Troubles 2 v. Verner's Pride 3 v. The Shadow of Ashlydyat 3 v. Trevlyn Hold 2 v. Lord Oak-

burn's Daughters 2 v. Oswald Cray 2 v. Mildred Arkell 2 v. St. Martin's Eve 2 v. Elster's Folly 2 v. Lady Adelaide's Oath 2 v. Orville College 1 v. A Life's Secret 1 v. The Red Court Farm 2 v. Anne Hereford 2 v. Roland Yorke 2 v. George Canterbury's Will 2 v. Bessy Rane 2 v. Dene Hollow 2 v. The Foggy Night at Offord, etc. 1 v. Within the Maze 2 v. The Master of Greylands 2 v. Johnny Ludlow (*First Series*) 2 v. Told in the Twilight 2 v. Adam Grainger 1 v. Edina 2 v. Pomeroy Abbey 2 v. Lost in the Post, etc. By Johnny Ludlow 1 v. A Tale of Sin, etc. By Johnny Ludlow 1 v. Anne, etc. By Johnny Ludlow 1 v. Court Netherleigh 2 v. The Mystery of Jessy Page, etc. By Johnny Ludlow 1 v. Helen Whitney's Wedding, etc. By Johnny Ludlow 1 v. The Story of Dorothy Grape, etc. By Johnny Ludlow 1 v.

Wordsworth: Select Poetical Works 2 v.

Lascelles Wraxall: Wild Oats 1 v.

Edm. Yates: Land at Last 2 v. Broken to Harness 2 v. The Forlorn Hope 2 v. Black Sheep 2 v. The Rock Ahead 2 v. Wrecked in Port 2 v. Dr. Wainwright's Patient 2 v. Nobody's Fortune 2 v. Castaway 2 v. A Waiting Race 2 v. The Yellow Flag 2 v. The Impending Sword 2 v. Two, by Tricks 1 v. A Silent Witness 2 v. Recollections and Experiences 2 v.

Miss Yonge: The Heir of Redclyffe 2 v. Heartsease 2 v. The Daisy Chain 2 v. Dynevor Terrace 2 v. Hopes and Fears 2 v. The Young Step-Mother 2 v. The Trial 2 v. The Clever Woman of the Family 2 v. The Dove in the Eagle's Nest 2 v. The Danvers Papers; the Prince and the Page 1 v. The Chaplet of Pearls 2 v. The two Guardians 1 v. The Caged Lion 2 v. The Pillars of the House 5 v. Lady Hester 1 v. My Young Alcides 2 v. The Three Brides 2 v. Womankind 2 v. Magnum Bonum 2 v. Love and Life 1 v. Unknown to History 2 v. Stray Pearls (w. portrait) 2 v. The Armourer's Prentices 2 v. The two Sides of the Shield 2 v.

Collection of German Authors.

B. Auerbach: On the Heights. Transl. by F. E. Bunnett. Second Authorized Edition, thoroughly revised, 3 v. Brigitta. From the German by C. Bell, 1 v. Spinoza. From the German by Nicholson, 2 v.

G. Ebers: An Egyptian Princess. Translated by E. Grove, 2 v. Uarda. From the German by Bell, 2 v. Homo Sum. From the German by Bell, 2 v. The Sisters. From the German by Bell, 2 v.

Fouqué: Undine, Sintram, etc. Translated by F. E. Bunnett, 1 v.

Ferdinand Freiligrath: Poems. From the German. Edited by his Daughter. Second Copyright Edition, enlarged, 1 v.

W. Görlach: Prince Bismarck (with Portrait). From the German by Miss M. E. von Glehn, 1 v.

Goethe: Faust. From the German by John Anster, LL. D. 1 v. Wilhelm Meister's Apprenticeship. From the German by Eleanor Grove, 2 v.

K. Gutzkow: Through Night to Light. From the German by M. A. Faber, 1 v.

F. W. Hackländer: Behind the Counter [Handel u. Wandel]. From the German by Howitt, 1 v.

W. Hauff: Three Tales. From the German by M. A. Faber, 1 v.

P. Heyse: L'Arrabiata and other Tales. From the German by M. Wilson, 1 v. The Dead Lake and other Tales. From the German by Mary Wilson, 1 v. Barbarossa and other Tales. From the German by L. C. S., 1 v.

Wilhelmine von Hillern: The Vulture Maiden [die Geier-Wally]. From the German by C. Bell and E. F. Poynter, 1 v. The Hour will come. From the German by Clara Bell, 2 v.

S. Kohn: Gabriel. A Story of the Jews in Prague. From the German by A. Milman, M.A., 1 v.

G. E. Lessing: Nathan the Wise and Emilia Galotti. The former transl. by W. Taylor, the latter by Chas. Lee Lewes, 1 v.

Fanny Lewald: Stella. From the German by Beatrice Marshall, 2 v.

E. Marlitt: The Princess of the Moor [das Haideprinzesschen], 2 v.

Maria Nathusius: Joachim von Kamern and Diary of a poor young Lady. From the German by Miss Thompson, 1 v.

Fritz Reuter: In the Year '13: Transl. from the Platt-Deutsch by Chas. Lee Lewes, 1 v. An old Story of my Farming Days [Ut mine Stromtid]. From the German by M. W. Macdowall, 3 v.

Jean Paul Friedr. Richter: Flower, Fruit and Thorn Pieces: or the Married Life, Death, and Wedding of the Advocate of the Poor, Firmian Stanislaus Siebenkäs. Translated from the German by E. H. Noel, 2 v

J. V. Scheffel: Ekkehard. A Tale of the tenth Century. Translated from the German by Sofie Delffs, 2 v.

G. Taylor: Klytia. From the German by Sutton Fraser Corkran, 2 v.

H. Zschokke: The Princess of Brunswick-Wolfenbüttel and other Tales. From the German by M. A. Faber, 1 v.

The price of each volume is 1 *Mark* 60 *Pfennige.*

Series for the Young.—*Each volume 1 Mark 60 Pf.*

Lady Barker: Stories About. With Frontispiece, 1 v.

Louisa Charlesworth: Ministering Children. With Frontispiece, 1 v.

Mrs. Craik (Miss Mulock): Our Year. Illustrated by C. Dobell, 1 v. Three Tales for Boys. With a Frontispiece by B. Plockhorst, 1 v. Three Tales for Girls. With a Frontispiece by B. Plockhorst, 1 v.

Miss G. M. Craik: Cousin Trix. With a Frontispiece by B. Plockhorst, 1 v.

Maria Edgeworth: Moral Tales. With a Frontispiece by B. Plockhorst, 1 v. Popular Tales. With a Frontispiece by B. Plockhorst, 2 v.

Bridget & Julia Kavanagh: The Pearl Fountain With a Frontispiece by B. Plockhorst, 1 v.

Charles and Mary Lamb: Tales from Shakspeare. With the Portrait of Shakspeare, 1 v.

Emma Marshall: Rex and Regina; or, The Song of the River. With six Illustrations, 1 vol.

Captain Marryat: Masterman Ready; or, the Wreck of the Pacific. With Frontispiece, 1 v.

Florence Montgomery: The Town-Crier; to which is added: The Children with the Indian-Rubber Ball, 1 v.

Ruth and her Friends. A Story for Girls. With Frontispiece, 1 v.

Mrs. Henry Wood: William Allair; or, Running away to Sea. Frontispiece from a Drawing by F. Gilbert, 1 v.

Miss Yonge: Kenneth; or, the Rear-Guard of the Grand Army. With Frontispiece, 1 v. The Little Duke. Ben Sylvester's Word. With a Frontispiece by B. Plockhorst, 1 v. The Stokesley Secret. With a Frontispiece by B. Plockhorst, 1 v. Countess Kate. With Frontispiece, 1 v. A Book of Golden Deeds. With a Frontispiece by B. Plockhorst, 2 v. Friarswood Post-Office. With Frontispiece, 1 v. Henrietta's Wish; or, Domineering. A Tale. With a Frontispiece by B. Plockhorst, 1 v. Kings of England: A History for the Young. With Frontispiece, 1 v. The Lances of Lynwood; the Pigeon Pie. With Frontispiece, 1 v. P's and Q's. With Frontispiece, 1 v. Aunt Charlotte's Stories of English History. With Frontispiece, 1 v. Bye-Words. With a Frontispiece by B. Plockhorst, 1 v. Lads and Lasses of Langley; Sowing and Sewing. With a Frontispiece by B. Plockhorst, 1 v.

Tauchnitz Manuals of Conversation.
Each bound ℳ 2,25.

Neues Handbuch der *Englischen* Conversationssprache von A. Schlessing.

A new Manual of the *German* Language of Conversation by A. Schlessing.

Neues Handbuch der *Französischen* Conversationssprache von L. Rollin.

Nouveau Manuel de la Conversation *Allemande* par MM. L. Rollin et Wolfgang Weber.

Tauchnitz Dictionaries.

A complete Dictionary of the English and German languages for general use. By *W. James*. Thirtieth Stereotype Edition. crown 8vo sewed Mark 4,50.

A complete Dictionary of the English and French languages for general use. By *W. James* and *A. Molé*. Thirteenth Stereotype Edition. crown 8vo sewed Mark 6,00.

A complete Dictionary of the English and Italian languages for general use. By *W. James* and *Gius. Grassi*. Ninth Stereotype Edition. crown 8vo sewed Mark 5,00.

A New Pocket Dictionary of the English and German languages. By *J. E. Wessely*. Twelfth Stereotype Edition. 16mo sewed Mark 1,50. bound Mark 2,25.

A New Pocket Dictionary of the English and French languages. By *J. E. Wessely*. Twelfth Stereotype Edition. 16mo sewed Mark 1,50. bound Mark 2,25.

A New Pocket Dictionary of the English and Italian languages. By *J. E. Wessely*. Tenth Stereotype Edition. 16mo sewed Mark 1,50. bound Mark 2,25.

A New Pocket Dictionary of the English and Spanish languages. By *J. E. Wessely* and *A. Gironés*. Ninth Stereotype Edition. 16mo sewed Mark 1,50. bound Mark 2,25.

A New Pocket Dictionary of the French and German languages. By *J. E. Wessely*. Third Stereotype Edition. 16mo sewed Mark 1,50. bound Mark 2,25.

A New Pocket Dictionary of the Italian and German languages. By *G. Locella*. Third Stereotype Edition. 16mo sewed Mark 1,50. bound Mark 2,25.

A New Dictionary of the Latin and English languages. Fifth Stereot. Ed. 16mo sewed Mark 1,50. bound Mark 2,25.

A New Pocket Dictionary of the French and Spanish languages. By *L. Tolhausen*. Stereotype Edition. 16mo sewed Mark 1,50. bound Mark 2,25.

Technological Dictionary in the French, English and German languages by *A. Tolhausen*. Revised by *L. Tolhausen*. Complete in three Parts, crown 8vo sewed Mark 26,00. Each Part separately: French, German, English [Third Edition, with a grand Supplement] Mark 10,00. (Grand Supplement separate Mark 3,00.) English, German, French [Second Edition, with a large Supplement] Mark 8,00. German, English, French [Second Edition] Mark 8,00.

A Hebrew and Chaldee Lexicon to the Old Testament. By Dr. *Julius Fürst*. Fifth Edition. Translated from the German by *Samuel Davidson*. Royal 8vo sewed Mark 19,00.

No orders of private purchasers are executed by the publisher.

BERNHARD TAUCHNITZ, LEIPZIG.

August 1885.

Tauchnitz Edition.

Latest Volumes:

Found Out. By Helen Mathers, 1 vol.

Near Neighbours. By Frances Mary Peard, 1 vol.

The Mystery of Jessy Page, etc. By Johnny Ludlow (Mrs. Henry Wood), 1 vol.

Letters to Guy, etc. By Lady Barker, 1 vol.

Affinities. By Mrs. Campbell Praed, 1 vol.

Although he was a Lord, etc. By Mrs. Forrester, 1 vol.

A History of the Four Georges. By Justin McCarthy, v. 1.

Wyllard's Weird. By M. E. Braddon, 3 vols.

Society in London. By a Foreign Resident, 1 vol.

A Maiden all Forlorn. By the Author of "Molly Bawn," 1 v.

A Little Tour in France. By Henry James, 1 vol.

Zoroaster. By F. Marion Crawford, 1 vol.

The Maritime Alps and their Seaboard. By the Author of "Vèra," 2 vols.

Helen Whitney's Wedding, etc. By Johnny Ludlow (Mrs. Henry Wood), 1 vol.

The Wise Women of Inverness. By William Black, 1 vol.

By Shore and Sedge. By Bret Harte, 1 vol.

Madame de Presnel. By E. Frances Poynter, 1 vol.

In the East Country. By Emma Marshall, 1 vol.

Cara Roma. By Miss Grant, 2 vols.

Corisande and other Tales. By Mrs. Forrester, 1 vol.

Ramona. By Helen Jackson, 2 vols.

Stella. By Fanny Lewald. From the German by Beatrice Marshall, 2 vols. (*German Authors.*)

Rex and Regina; or, The Song of the River. By E. Marshall. With six Illustrations, 1 vol. (*Series for the Young.*)

A complete Catalogue of the Tauchnitz Edition is attached to this work.

Bernhard Tauchnitz, Leipzig;

2153993R00157

Printed in Great Britain
by Amazon.co.uk, Ltd.,
Marston Gate.